Also by Tim Kreider

The Pain—When Will It End?
Why Do They Kill Me?
Twilight of the Assholes

We Learn Nothing

Essays and Cartoons

Tim Kreider

FREE PRESS

NEW YORK   LONDON   TORONTO   SYDNEY   NEW DELHI

*f*P

Free Press
A Division of Simon & Schuster, Inc.
1230 Avenue of the Americas
New York, NY 10020

First Free Press hardcover edition June 2012

FREE PRESS and colophon are trademarks of Simon & Schuster, Inc.

For information about special discounts for bulk purchases, please contact Simon & Schuster Special Sales at 1-866-506-1949 or business@simonandschuster.com.

The Simon & Schuster Speakers Bureau can bring authors to your live event. For more information or to book an event contact the Simon & Schuster Speakers Bureau at 1-866-248-3049 or visit our website at www.simonspeakers.com.

Designed by Akasha Archer

The following essays first appeared, in different form, on www.nytimes.com: "Reprieve," "You Can't Stay Here" (as "Time and the Bottle"), "How They Tried to Fuck Me Over" (as "Isn't It Outrageous?"), "The Referendum," and "Averted Vision."

"The Stabbing Story" was originally published in *The Urbanite*.

All of these cartoons first appeared in the Baltimore *City Paper*. "What's Your Plan (When the Shit Hits the Fan)" also appears in *Twilight of the Assholes*, and is reprinted here with the kind permission of Fantagraphics Books. All illustrations are original.

Manufactured in the United States of America

10   9   8   7   6   5   4   3   2   1

Library of Congress Cataloging-in-Publication Data

Kreider, Tim.
We learn nothing: essays and cartoons / Tim Kreider
p. cm.
1. American wit and humor. I. Title.
PN6165.K75 2012
814'. 6—dc23   2011050095

ISBN 978-1-4391-9870-4
ISBN 978-1-4391-9872-8 (ebook)

For my mother and father

Author's Note

Most of the names of people mentioned in these essays (except for those of my colleagues, Jennifer Boylan, Sarah Glidden, and Matt, aka "Slim Dodger"), as well as certain other identifying details, have been changed. Nothing else has been made up.

When Reinhold Messner returned from the first solo climb of Everest, he was severely dehydrated, and utterly exhausted; he fell down most of the last part of the descent, and collapsed on the Rongbuk glacier, and he was crawling over it on hands and knees when the woman who was his entire support team reached him; and he looked up at her out of a delirium, and said, "Where are all my friends?"

—Kim Stanley Robinson, *Red Mars*

Contents

Contents

We Learn Nothing

Reprieve

Fourteen years ago, I was stabbed in the throat. This is kind of a long story and less interesting than it sounds. A lot of people have told me about their own near-death experiences over the years, often in harrowing medical detail, imagining that those details— how many times they rolled the car, how many vertebrae shattered, how many months spent in traction—will somehow convey the subjective psychic force of the experience, the way some people will relate the whole narrative of a dream in a futile attempt to evoke its ambient feeling. Except for the ten or fifteen minutes during which it looked like I was about to die, which I would prefer not to relive, getting stabbed wasn't even among the worst experiences of my life. In fact it was one of the best things that ever happened to me.

After my unsuccessful murder I wasn't unhappy for an entire year. Winston Churchill's aphorism about the exhilaration of being shot at without result is verifiably true. I was reminded of an old Ray Bradbury story, "The Lost City of Mars," in which a man finds a miraculous machine that enables him to experience his own violent death over and over again, as many times as he likes—in locomotive collisions, race car crashes, exploding rocket ships—until he emerges flayed of all his Christian guilt and unconscious longing for death, forgiven and free, finally alive.

I can't claim to have been continuously euphoric the whole time; it's just that, during that grace period, nothing much could bother me or get me down. The horrible thing that I'd always dreaded was going to happen to me had finally happened. I figured I was off the hook for a while. In a parallel universe only two millimeters away—the distance between my carotid and the stiletto—I had been flown home in the cargo hold instead of in coach. As far as I was concerned everything in this life was what Raymond Carver, in writing of his own second chance, called "gravy."

My friends immediately mocked me out of my self-consciousness about the nerve damage that had left me with a lopsided smile. I started brewing my own dandelion wine in a big Amish crock. I listened to old one-hit wonders much too stupid to name in print. And I developed a strange new laugh that's stayed with me to this day—a raucous, barking thing that comes from deep in the dia-phragm, the laugh of a much larger man, that makes people in bars or restaurants look over for a second to make sure I'm not about to open up on the crowd with a weapon. I don't laugh this way all the time—certainly not when I'm just being polite. The last time it happened was when I told my friend Harold, "You don't un-derstand me," in mock-wounded protest at some unjust charge of sleazery, and he retorted: "No, sir, I understand you very well—it is you who do not understand yourself." The laugh always seems to be in response to the same elusive joke, some dark, hilarious universal truth.

Not for one passing moment did it occur to me to imagine that God Must Have Spared My Life for Some Purpose. Even if I'd been the type who was prone to such silly notions, I would've been rudely disabused of it by the heavy-handed coincidence of the Oklahoma City bombing occurring on the same day I spent in a coma. If there is some divine plan that requires my survival and the deaths of all those children in day care, I respectfully decline to participate. What I had been was not blessed or chosen but lucky.

Not to turn up my nose at luck; it's better to be lucky than just about anything else in life. And if you're reading this now you're among the lucky, too.

I wish I could recommend the experience of not being killed to everyone. It's a truism that this is why people enjoy thrill-seeking pastimes, ranging from harmless adrenaline fixes like horror movies and roller coasters to what are essentially suicide attempts with safety nets, like bungee jumping and skydiving. The trick is that to get the full effect you have to be genuinely uncertain that you're going to survive. The best approximation would be to hire an incompetent, Clouseauesque hit man to assassinate you.

It's one of the maddening perversities of human psychology that we only notice we're alive when we're reminded we're going to die, the same way some of us appreciate our girlfriends only after they've become exes. I saw the same thing happen, in a more profound and lasting way, to my father when he was terminally ill: a lightening, an amused indifference to the nonsense that the rest of us think of as the serious business of the world. A neighbor was suing my father over some property dispute during his illness, but if you tried to talk to him about such practical matters he'd just sing you old songs like "A Bird in a Gilded Cage" in a silly, quavering falsetto until you gave up. He cared less about things that didn't matter and more about the things that did. It was during his illness that he gave me the talk that all my artist friends have envied, in which he told me that he and my mother believed in my talent and I shouldn't worry about getting "some dumb job."

Maybe people who have lived with the reality of their own mortality for months or years are permanently changed by it, but getting stabbed was more like getting struck by lightning, over almost as soon as it happened, and the illumination didn't last. You can't feel crazily grateful to be alive your whole life any more than you can stay passionately in love forever—or grieve forever, for that matter. Time makes us all betray ourselves and get back to the busywork of living. Before a year had gone by, the same everyday anxieties and frustrations began creeping back. I was disgusted to catch myself yelling in traffic, pounding on my computer, lying awake at night worrying about what was to become of me. I can't recapture that feeling of euphoric gratitude any more than I can really remember the mortal terror I felt when I was pretty sure I had about four minutes to live. But I know that it really happened, that that state of grace is accessible to us, even if I only blundered across it once and never find my way back. At my cabin on the Chesapeake Bay I'll see bald eagles swoop up from the water with wriggling little fish in their talons, and whenever they accidentally drop their catch, I like to imagine that fish trying to tell his friends about his own near-death experience, a perspective so unprecedented there are no words in the fish language to describe it: for a short time he was outside the world, he could see forever, there's so much more than they knew, but he's glad to be back.

Once a year on my stabbiversary, I remind myself that this is still my bonus life, a round on the house. But now that I'm back in the slog of everyday life, I have to struggle to keep things in what I still insist is their true perspective. I know intellectually that all the urgently pressing items on our mental lists—our careers, car repairs, the daily headlines, the goddamned taxes—are just so much noise, that what matters is spending time with the people you love. It's just hard to bear in mind when the hard drive crashes or the shower drain clogs first thing in the day. Apparently I can only ever attain that God's-eye view in the grip of the talons.

I was not cheered to read about psychological studies suggesting that most people inevitably return to a certain emotional baseline after circumstantial highs and lows. How happy we can hope to be may be as inalterable and unfair as our height or metabolism or the age at which we'll lose our hair. This is reassuring news if you've undergone some trauma, but less so if your own emotional thermostat is set so low it makes you want to phone up the landlord and yell at him. You'd like to think that nearly getting killed would be a permanently life-altering experience, but in truth it was less painful, and occasioned less serious reflection, than certain break-ups I've gone through. I've demonstrated an impressive resilience in the face of valuable life lessons, and the main thing I seem to have learned from this one is that I am capable of learning nothing from almost any experience, no matter how profound. If anything, the whole episode only confirmed my solipsistic suspicion that in the story of Me only supporting characters would die, while I, its first-person narrator and star, was immortal. It gave me much more of an existential turn when my vision started to blur.

I don't know why we take our worst moods so much more seriously than our best, crediting depression with more clarity than euphoria. We dismiss peak moments and passionate love affairs as an ephemeral chemical buzz, just endorphins or hormones, but accept those 3 A.M. bouts of despair as unsentimental insights into the truth about our lives. It's easy now to dismiss that year as nothing more than the same sort of shaky, hysterical high you'd feel after getting clipped by a taxi. But you could also try to think of it as a glimpse of reality, being jolted out of a lifelong stupor. It's like the revelation I had the first time I ever flew in an airplane as a kid: when you break through the cloud cover you realize that above the passing squalls and doldrums there is a realm of eternal sunlight, so keen and brilliant you have to squint against it, a vision to hold on to when you descend once again beneath the clouds, under the oppressive, petty jurisdiction of the local weather.

The Stabbing Story

There's a crucial phase early in the telling of a story when it's still fluid; it hasn't yet coalesced into its canonical form. You're still fixing the best details, eliding certain boring or inconvenient facts, learning how to structure and time it for effect. You're still figuring out what *kind* of story it is — comic, or dramatic, or tragic, or what.

Right before they put me under I stopped the surgeon and asked him, 'So can I expect to wake up?'

He sort of smiled and shrugged and said, 'Sure.'

STILL QUITE LURID

I wrote a great version to my friend Aaron from my hospital bed in Crete. It began:

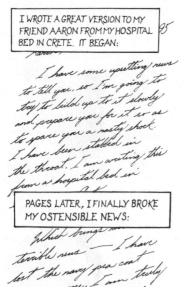

> I have some upsetting news to tell you, so I'm going to try to build up to it slowly and prepare you for it so as to spare you a nasty shock. I have been stabbed in the throat. I am writing this from a hospital bed in

PAGES LATER, I FINALLY BROKE MY OSTENSIBLE NEWS:

> Which brings me terrible news — I have lost the navy pea coat you gave me. I am truly sorry. I had it on when I told me to the ER in

I custom-designed a version to tell my mother long-distance — a masterpiece of preemption, carefully constructed to afford her no opening in which to panic.

First of all, I'm fine, but I wanted to let you know that I'm in the hospital. I—

WHAT? OH, WHAT HAPPEN...?!

Well, what happened was, I suffered an injury, but—

OH MY?! I'M MY!! OH MY?!?!

Oh — um, technically a stab wound? I actually got stabbed? but—

WHAT?! NO!!

Oh, in the, uh, neck area, but — NO but the important thing is that I AM FINE.

MOM LATER TOLD ME SHE'D CALMLY ABSORBED THIS INFORMATION, GONE BACK TO SLEEP, THEN WOKE UP A FEW HOURS LATER AND FREAKED OUT.

I DEVELOPED TWO DIFFERENT VERSIONS: THE LONG VERSION, WHICH INCLUDED MY OBSESSIVE SEARCH FOR VIETNAM NOVELIST GUSTAV HASFORD, WHO'D GONE TO GREECE TO DRINK HIMSELF TO DEATH—A WHOLE JUNGIAN ODYSSEY INTO DEATH AND REBIRTH!

I NEVER TELL THIS VERSION ANYMORE.

...AND THERE WAS THE SHORT VERSION, FOR CASUAL ACQUAINTANCES: JUST A STORY OF RANDOM VIOLENCE.

THE ROLE OF THE GIRL INVOLVED CHANGED CONSIDERABLY FROM EARLY DRAFTS, ESPECIALLY AFTER SHE TRIED TO MOVE IN WITH ME.

MY TELLING OF THE STORY REACHED ITS MOST PERFECT REFINEMENT THE TIME I TOLD IT IN FRONT OF MY FRIEND ANNIE — WHO HAD ALREADY HEARD IT, AND FAMOUSLY CARES FOR NO ONE BUT HERSELF — AND IT MADE HER WEEP.

THE DOCTORS TOLD ME IT WAS TWO MILLIMETERS FROM MY CAROTID ARTERY.

HOLY CRAP, DUDE.

(ANNIE ALSO WEEPS AT THE THEME FROM "THE INCREDIBLE HULK.")

EVENTUALLY IT GOT FORMALIZED AND BORING FOR ME, THE WAY A PERFORMANCE GOES STALE.

AFTER A FEW YEARS I REALIZED THAT I WAS NEVER GOING TO BE DONE TELLING THIS STORY. AS LONG AS I KEPT MEETING PEOPLE, I WOULD ALWAYS HAVE TO TELL IT AGAIN.

...YEAH, IT WAS ACTUALLY TWO MILLIMETERS FROM MY CAROTID ARTERY.

OH MY GOD.

JESUS WHAT HAPPENED TO YOUR NECK?

HM?

(ADMITTEDLY, STILL PRETTY LIVID)

EVENTUALLY I TOOK TO LETTING OTHER PEOPLE TELL IT FOR ME.
I ESPECIALLY ENJOYED HEARING MY FRIEND ALEX'S VERSION.

I KEEL YOU!

...WEREN'T YOU RESCUING A PROSTITUTE FROM, LIKE, HER LIFE OF SIN?

SURE. YES!

BY NOW I'VE TOLD IT SO MANY TIMES THAT IT'S HARD TO SEPARATE THE STORY FROM THE REALITY—LIKE THOSE CHILDHOOD MEMORIES THAT ARE REALLY ONLY MEMORIES OF HEARING THE STORY TOLD.

"Meeting Walt Disney at an airport, ca. 1970."

*WALT DISNEY. d. DECEMBER 1966; ME, b. FEBRUARY 1967.

THESE DAYS, WHEN PEOPLE SAY:

HEY CAN I JUST ASK YOU— HOW'D YOU GET THAT SCAR?

I GENERALLY ANSWER,

I'M A... AFRAI...

IT'S KIND OF A LONG STORY.

How to Win Her Back

"THE CLASSIC": SEND HER AN EAR!

...BOTH EARS, MAYBE?

...TOO MUCH?

"THE HINCKLEY" SHOOT THE PRESIDENT.

STILL THE ONLY PRESIDENT WORTH SHOOTING.

"PER ASPERA AD AMOR": PUT ON AN ADULT DIAPER, GET IN THE CAR AND GO.

SURE-FIRE: CREATE A WORK OF ART INSPIRED BY HER!

(THE LADIES CANNOT RESIST.)

The Creature Walks Among Us

A few years ago an astronaut who'd been jilted in a romantic space triangle reportedly donned an adult diaper and drove hundreds of miles across the country, armed with pepper spray, a knife, and a BB pistol, to confront her rival.* The news media got a week's worth of fun out of that story; the national consensus amounted to those middle school sneers, "What*ever*" and "O-kaaaayyyy. . . ." Everyone was eager to laugh at that unhappy woman to reassure themselves that she was crazy, her behavior incomprehensible. But I knew exactly how she felt.

I had a perhaps unhealthy empathy for that astronaut because, as it happened, around the same time she undertook her own mission, I'd nearly driven twenty hours for similar reasons. Not to abduct anyone, of course, ha ha, no, certainly not—just to make a desperate last-ditch appeal. The object of my obsession was on vacation somewhere on the Carolina shore, and I vaguely pictured myself kneeling in the surf, shocking the moms and toddlers around us. I actually got in the car and sat in the driveway with my hands on the hot steering wheel, poised to launch. What stayed me

---

* That astronaut's lawyer was at pains to dispute the diaper claim, which seems like a curious detail to fixate on, given the other items in her possession.

was not any awareness that this might be alarming or delusional behavior, but only the concern that it might backfire and drive the person in question further away from me. At such moments it never occurs to you to question your loyalty to the Acme brand, much less ask yourself whether it's really worth all this trouble and personal injury to try to catch one scrawny roadrunner; your only hesitation is in choosing between the rocket skates or the earth-quake pills. I could understand that donning the diaper was not insane but exactly the sort of thoroughness and resourcefulness that NASA inculcates in its astronaut corps. When love is at stake, you do not waste time on rest stops.

There's a fine line between the bold romantic gesture and stalk-ing. The tricky crux of the matter is that it depends to a great extent on how that gesture is going to be received—which factor, unfor-tunately, the impetuous suitor/obsessed stalker has lost all ability to gauge. A friend of mine reports that all the women he's polled have been enthusiastic advocates of the bold romantic gesture, but this, he suspects, is because they're all automatically picturing John Cu-sack making it, not Steve Buscemi or Peter Lorre or the Creature from the Black Lagoon. Often you don't know whether you're the hero of a romantic comedy or the villain on a Lifetime special until the restraining order arrives.

That astronaut's official NASA photo and her police mug shot make for instructive before-and-after illustrations of the effects of love, as grimly cautionary as ad campaigns about the ravages of crystal meth. I was moved to unpleasant recognition by that photo of her face—gaunt and disheveled, deranged, exhausted, utterly broken and lost. I had seen that face before, in the mirror. And so, I bet, have most of us. We've just been lucky enough not to have it photographed for the public record. But we shouldn't let our-selves forget it, or the weeks or months we spent curled up weep-ing on the couch, smashing glassware, kicking through drywall, sending ill-advised emails and having wrenching late-night phone conversations, watching whole seasons of TV series at one sitting, listening to the one song we could still bear to hear over and over again, planning impulsive romantic proposals or scheming terrible revenge. We've all worn the diaper.

I'm as cheered as anyone when some crusader for family values is caught in a cheap motel, a defender of traditional marriage arrested in a men's room, or some censorious guardian of the children has his laptop confiscated. But I can't quite bring myself to join in the smirking over more ordinary lechery and weakness— a former governor mooning over his "soul mate" at a press conference, a talk-show host confessing on the air to affairs with his interns.* Whom, exactly, do we think we're kidding? Is all this solemn reproach and pretended incomprehension just for the benefit of prigs and evangelicals, the same way movies have to be hilariously bowdlerized on TV for the sake of viewers under ten? The usual rationale for our nosy interest in the private disgraces of public figures is that they show poor judgment, but this is like charging kamikazes with poor navigation; these transgressions take place in a realm beyond judgment. The truth is, people are ravenous for sex, sociopaths for love. I sometimes like to daydream that if we were all somehow simultaneously outed as lechers and perverts and sentimental slobs, it might be, after the initial shock of disillusionment, liberating. It might be a relief to quit maintaining this rigid pose of normalcy and own up to the outlaws and monsters we are.

Whenever I have to listen to the media's priggish tittering over the latest sex scandal, I feel like a closeted homosexual having to

---

*By the time you read this, these stories will be as old as the Nan Britton scandal or Fatty Arbuckle trials, but new faces will have replaced theirs in the national pillory.

smile tightly through his coworker's jokes about fags. I've had the kind of romantic life that would give a biographer a lot to work with, punctuated by passionate and disastrous affairs. I enjoyed reading about H. G. Wells, who was an early advocate of free love and contraception and a very sloppy practitioner of both. His biography is full of lurid scandals like the one in which a pregnant young lover slashed her wrists in his study, obliging him to flee to the Continent while it all blew over. (I've often wished for a Continent to flee to.) It's easy to forget that such lives are more fun to read about than to live. Biographies tend to focus on the delirious highs, like Ava Gardner and Frank Sinatra tossing empty champagne bottles out of their convertible and shooting out street lights with a pistol on their first date, and elide the years when the subject lies alone in bed drinking and watching her own old movies on late-night TV. The goal of a life is not to provide material for good stories. Because it must also be noted that I've spent a larger percentage of my life than any sane person would wish crouching on the bathroom floor sobbing into a smelly old towel.

Heartbreak is the common term for this condition—a Hallmark euphemism for something that's about as romantic as pancreatitis. I've endured three or four let's call them episodes in my life. Which may not seem like all that many unless you're a friend of mine who's had to watch. I would not want to relive even one second of those times, nor would I wish them on anyone else, but I also don't know if I can relate to anyone who hasn't gone through them. (I respect people who had to quit drinking lest it kill them, but those who never saw the appeal of the stuff in the first place seem not quite to be trusted.) At such times we are certainly not at our best but we are undeniably at our most human—utterly vulnerable, naked and laid open, a mess.

Whenever I overhear someone talking on a cell phone about an illicit affair or excruciating divorce, or read the anguished confessions on postsecret.com or the hopeless mash notes in the "missed connections" ads, it feels like a glimpse into the secret history of the world. It belies the consensual pretense that the main thing going on in this life is work and the making of money. I love it when passion rips open that dull nine-to-five façade and bares the writhing orgy of need underneath. Seeing someone working at her laptop in a coffee shop, you construct a fantasy of her as smart, hardheaded, and competent—All Business—but then when her girlfriend arrives she pours out the same old story of crushed-out delusion, drunken flirting, mixed signals, and trick questions. It thrilled me to overhear my postmaster, whom I'd never imagined as a Byronic hero, saying mournfully into the phone: "Shelly and me never meant for anything to happen. It just happened." Listen to some country songs, the music of the heartland, that alleged bastion of family values: lachrymose ballads about loving the wrong man, killing your wife in a jealous rage, truckers and waitresses suffering Shakespearian torments, torn between passion and virtue.

My friend Lauren once told me that she could totally understand—which is not the same as sympathize with—those losers who kill their exes and/or their exes' new lovers, that black, annihilating If-I-can't-have-her-then-no-one-else-will impulse, because it's so painful to know that the person you love is still out there in the world, living their life, going to work and laughing with friends and drinking margaritas. It's a lesser hurt than grief, but, in a way, crueler—it's more like being dead yourself, and having to watch life go on without you. I loved her for owning up to this. Not that Lauren or I—or you—would ever do any such thing ourselves. But I sometimes wonder whether the line between those of us who don't do such things and the few who do is as impermeable as we like to think. Anytime I hear about another one of us gone berserk, shooting up his ex's office or drowning her kids to free herself up for her Internet boyfriend, the question I always ask is not, like every other tongue-clucking pundit in the country, *how could this have happened?* but *why doesn't this happen every day?* It makes me proud of all of us who are secretly going to pieces behind closed doors but still somehow keeping it together for the public, collaborating in the shaky ongoing effort of not letting civilization fall apart for one more day.

This kind of anarchic, Dionysian love doesn't give a shit about commitments or institutions; it smashes our illusions about what kind of people we are, what we would and would not do, exposing the difference between what we *want* to want and what we really want. We may choose friendships based on common interests and complementary qualities, but our reasons for falling in love are altogether more irrational, projections of our most infantile wants and pathology. (Lovers know that it feels less as if they've chosen each other than as if they've both been chosen by something else.) Seeing the people our friends are attracted to often illuminates aspects of their personalities we don't recognize. Sometimes it reveals something unexpectedly beautiful, as when a driven careerist marries a feckless artist, or a glamorous woman mentions that her first boyfriend was disfigured. But sometimes the things we learn about them are things we would've preferred not to see. Their voices change around their lovers in ways that make us cringe to hear. A lot of couples look disturbingly alike. (I remember meeting one couple who I at first assumed were identical twins until I saw them kiss. It somehow seemed like a depressing indictment of our whole species' capacity for loving anything even slightly other than ourselves, as well as negating the whole point of the last billion years of sexual reproduction. Why not just bud like hydras if we're going to mate with our doubles?) Our lovers are summoned up by the most primal and naked parts of ourselves. Introducing these people to our friends and family is, in a way, more heedlessly exhibitionistic than posting nude photos or sex tapes of ourselves online; it's like letting everyone watch our uncensored dreams.

I have watched my female friends' reactions as they've met some of my girlfriends. I could see them thinking: *Really?* (People of the same gender, or impartial sexual orientation, can see more easily through the camouflage of beauty.) These friends are like my sisters; they know me well and love me, and I respect their opinions and trust their judgment. And yet, on those occasions, I smiled defiantly into their eyes, beaming the telepathic message back at them: *It doesn't matter what you think.* Later they would get to hold me as I wept. There's no reasoning with someone in this state: your best option is to cold-cock him and dump him on a boat bound for Hong Kong with a note pinned to his shirt: *Sorry. Doing you a favor. Thank me later.* I've known so many people who claimed to be happy in relationships in which, to the outside observer, they appeared to be miserable. When they finally broke up with their beloved antagonists they described themselves as bereft, even though to everyone around them they seemed possessed of new energy, health, and good humor. What the people in these relationships are is not "happy"; it's something more necessary than happiness, for which we don't have a word in our language.

I have known some people who selected their mates on the same bases on which they chose friends: affinity, compatibility, common goals. I like to believe that these people are innocent of true passion, that they haven't yet met the person for whom they would forfeit everything. What I fear they actually are is emotionally healthy. I have one friend who had a history, in adolescence and early adulthood, of attractions to brilliant, self-absorbed, alcoholic men, and after one especially damaging relationship she simply decided never to get involved with that kind of man again, and married someone altogether different. I find this admirable, but it is also alien to me. I recently met a very difficult but beautiful ex-girlfriend for coffee, and as we were talking I had two epiphanies: 1) I do not even like this person and yet 2) I would sneak off to the bathroom with her right now. With some people, it's all a foregone conclusion once you get close enough to inhale the scent of their hair.

I have loved women who were saner and kinder than me, for whom I became the best version of myself. But it's also a relief to be with someone who's *not* better than you, who's just as bad and likes it. With these women, I didn't have to impersonate a better person than myself; we were complicit, accomplices. They each had a streak of reckless selfishness, a readiness to wreck everything. One threw her mother's fifteen-thousand-dollar engagement ring into a mountain lake in token of her vow never again to submit to monogamy. Another I will always remember in afternoon barlight as she suddenly swept a tableful of peanut shells onto the sawdust floor, crying "Hah!" with lusty abandon. I had to turn my face away; I knew then that we were in too far to back out. It was like that floating, slow-motion moment before the roller coaster begins its heady, accelerating descent. I still have a piece of art that another lover bought for me, a cartoon by one J. W. Banks showing two hapless characters in a single-propeller plane that's hurtling earthward, streaming flames: "Oh my God forgive me I've lieded," the one in the pilot's seat confesses aloud. "Mo, I never flew one of these things before. I forgot our chute's and we going to crash." His comrade Mo, to whom this is all clearly news, clutches the sides of the cockpit, his mouth popped open in a comical little *O?!* of alarm. It was meant as a rueful joke; we still thought we knew very well that we didn't know what we were doing, what kind of dangerous contraption we'd gotten ourselves into. We adored feeling out of control, the intoxication of free fall. We didn't know yet how far down it was.

Even in the midst of these deliriums, some tiny, invincibly sane part of my brain, like the last surviving scholar barricaded in the library of a burning city, realized that the intensity of emotion I was experiencing was disproportionate to my actual investment in these relationships. I spent a summer racked with loss over a woman with whom I'd had only four weekends and a lot of phone calls, which we mostly spent listening to each other breathe. I wasted a year of my life torturing myself with jealousy and rage over someone I knew I didn't want to be with; what I wanted was not to lose her. That passion took these women as its objects as arbitrarily, and as indispensably, as a fetish fixates on an elbow or stiletto or a bathtub full of flan. Those emotional cataclysms were not only incommensurate to the circumstances but felt much bigger than I was, like a lightning strike channeled through a 60-watt bulb. I knew—not that it helped—that this must be some awful abreaction, erupting from someplace deeper inside me than I knew I went. I was like a luckless hiker blown apart by old unexploded ordnance from a war he'd never even heard of. Anyone who's read Freud or spent time in therapy or just listened to call-in radio shows knows that these episodes are reenactments of old infantile melodramas, unexorcised abandonments or betrayals. (The imperious fury I felt at these breakups was like nothing else I've ever experienced in adulthood, but anyone who's heard an infant waking up alone in the night would recognize the howling.) The trick, I suppose, is to find someone with a touch of the pathology you require, but not so much that it will destroy you. But, as with drinking just enough to feel mellow and well-disposed toward the world, but not so much that you end up vomiting in the street, this can take some trial and error to calibrate.

These erotic addictions have only occasionally overlapped with, or unexpectedly become, what I'd call love. Love tends to sneak up on me over a period of years, and had less the quality of some transfiguring vision than of simple recognition, like suddenly seeing the answer to a puzzle that's been obvious all along. Someone shows you the rabbit's foot she just bought, explaining, "It was the last green one," or simply reaches out and takes your lapel to steady herself as the subway decelerates into the station, and you realize: *Uh-oh.* Even though those breakups and disentanglements hurt, and it may always make me a little sad to see those women, they are the ones I will love for life, the ones I'd want to have by my deathbed. The kind of bond I feel with the women I've fallen so horribly in love with is more involuntary, as arbitrary and indissoluble as the one that unites the survivors of some infamous disaster. One of my former lovers proposed having T-shirts made as souvenirs for all the participants in/casualties of our affair that would read *Armageddon '97.* She finds this funnier than I do.

It came as a belated epiphany to me when I learned that the Greeks had several different words for the disparate phenomena that in English we indiscriminately lump together under the label *love.* Our inability to distinguish between, say, *eros* (sexual love) and *storgé* (the love that grows out of friendship) leads to more than semantic confusion. Careening through this world with such a crude taxonomical guide to human passion is as foolhardy as piloting a plane ignorant of the difference between *stratus* and *cumulonimbus,* knowing only the word *cloud.*

I don't know whether I would trade in those dizzying highs to rid myself of the memory of the crashes and wreckage. About the best thing I got out of any of those affairs was a really good pie crust recipe. But if anyone were to ask me, "Have you ever been in love?" I could at least say, with the same sort of rueful pride as a recovering alcoholic who's asked whether he's ever been known to take a drink: "Oh, yes." I've known kisses so narcotic they made my eyes roll back in my head. For a few weeks one winter I walked around feeling like I had a miniature sun in my heart. I learned that making out on the subway is one of those things, like smoking cigars or riding Jet-Skis, that is obnoxious and repulsive when other people do it but incredibly fun when it is you. And there are still songs that, whenever I hear them, whatever I'm doing, will send me into a moment's exquisite reverie, like an old injury's twinge at an oncoming storm. Maybe one reason artists seems so susceptible to love affairs is that being in love is one of the only times when life is anything like art—when we actually feel the way torch songs and arias sound, the way Gene Kelly looks singing in the rain. It might all have been worth it if I'd been the only one hurt.

A few years ago my friend Kevin, who'd just spent a month in the hospital after a heart attack, gave it to me straight: "You gotta stop being heartbroken all the time. I gotta stop being a big fat slob who almost dies." For both of us it meant giving up some beloved vices. Neither of us is exactly practiced at renunciation, or even moderation, so we've both had the occasional backslide—I'll have a fling with a grad student/lap dancer or he'll eat an entire clam pizza and collapse. But for the most part we're both being more cautious of our hearts.

Right now I'm neither in love nor heartbroken. I almost hesitate to say this: it still feels provisional, like remission. Sometimes I'm afraid it may be as ephemeral as that temporary sanity that afflicts us for as long as forty-five seconds after orgasm. But at other times I worry it may be permanent. Maybe we have a finite capacity for falling in love that gets depleted with age. Or maybe romantic love is an affliction of adolescence, like acne or a passionate ideological investment in pop songs. It's mostly a relief to be free of it, like not waking up hung over. At those moments when I've felt myself starting to relapse—waiting for someone to call who wasn't going to, that familiar helplessness clutching my gut—I've recoiled like a recovering alcoholic waking from a dream of being blacked-out drunk, relieved and thankful that he's still sober.

But sometimes this life starts to feel grudging and dutiful. I'm clear-eyed again, but the world looks lusterless and dull. I can understand why schizophrenics stop taking their meds. I'm functioning and accomplishing things; everyone approves of my behavior and agrees that I seem happier; I'm not embarrassing my friends with any histrionic displays. But I also know that all around me the air is full of songs too beautiful for me to hear. Sometimes I'll see a pair of electric-blue damselflies coupled in flight, and I remember how it felt to be weightless.

The Road to Recovery

SPEND TIME WITH GOOD FRIENDS.

DO THE THINGS YOU ENJOY!

REBOUND SEX!

AND REMEMBER: TIME HEALS ALL WOUNDS.

MY WORST ENEMY—
Past Tim

LIKE A BAD ROOMMATE, HE ROUTINELY
LEAVES THE GROUNDS IN THE FRENCH PRESS

STAYS OUT LATE DRINKING WHEN HE *KNOWS*
I HAVE A CARTOON TO DRAW THE NEXT DAY

APPARENTLY JUST GOOFED OFF
FOR THE LAST TWENTY YEARS

MOST FRUSTRATING OF ALL, HE REMAINS
FOREVER BEYOND THE REACH OF JUSTICE—
THE ONLY ONE I CAN PUNISH IS... *FUTURE TIM.*

You Can't Stay Here

My years of heavy drinking were roughly coterminous with my youth, and it's difficult, in retrospect, to tell which of them I really miss. The association between the two is not just a Pavlovian one. Drunkenness and youth share in a certain reckless irresponsibility, and the illusion of timelessness. The young and the drunk are both temporarily exempt from that oppressive sense of obligation that ruins so much of our lives, the nagging worry that we really ought to be doing something productive instead. It's the illicit savor of time stolen, time knowingly and joyfully squandered. There's more than one reason we call it being "wasted."

Of course time doesn't stop for anyone; alcohol just keeps you from feeling it, the way it'll keep a man cozy while he freezes to death. It elides the years as painlessly as it does hours; your twenties turn into your thirties the same way you'll look at your watch one minute and it's only 8:30—the night is young, all the time in the world—and then suddenly and without warning it's last call. I found myself unexpectedly in my forties in much the same way I used to wake up disoriented on friends' couches. I'm a little appalled by all the time I've lost. I don't feel middle-aged—I just feel like I've been young a lot longer than most people. This lifestyle also leaves you with some conspicuous gaps on your résumé that can be hard to explain in job interviews. I now regret never having played hooky from school, not least because if I had I might not have felt compelled to play hooky from life for the next twenty years. Because it turns out that you can blow life off for as long as you want, but you still have to take the finals.

But then, wasting time wasn't exactly an unforeseen side effect of drinking; it was part of the fun. Of course it was fun; if drinking weren't so much fun it wouldn't be such a widespread and terrible problem. While responsible people were working their way up their respective professional ladders, my friends and I were spending whole days drinking bottomless pitchers of mimosas or Bloody Marys and laughing till we wept on decks overlooking the Chesapeake Bay. There used to be a bar located in one of New York City's subway stations, where you could sit on a ratty old sofa drinking cans of Pabst watching the rush hour commuters stream past the doorway. Once in a while one of them would notice you there out of the corner of his eye, and for an instant you'd see him register the improbable vision you presented, like a glimpse of himself in a parallel universe. There is no drinking as enjoyable as daytime drinking, when the sun is out, the bars are empty of dilettantes, and the afternoon stretches ahead of you like summer vacation. The gleeful complicity you and your friends share in the excellent decision to have one more round, knowing full well you're forfeiting the rest of the day (*You know what? I can catch a later train*)—you can almost physically feel something lifted from you at this moment, even if you know, on some level, that it will fall back more heavily later on. My friend Nick used to raise the toast: "Gentlemen—our lives are unbelievably great."

This bargain was not without typical satanic subclauses: you get to have far more fun than most sober people ever do, but you don't get to remember it. I could tell you a few hundred hilarious anecdotes about those days, but the exact chronology of events gets a little hazy for a couple of decades. Nick and I once wrecked our friend Gabe's entire dining room laughing at something one of us had said, whirling around and toppling over and clutching desperately at tablecloths and knickknack shelves, like a couple of robots gone berserk, but the next morning neither of us could remember what had been so funny. It's gone, irretrievable, and, like lost masterpieces, it's become enshrined in our imaginations as an unsurpassable ideal, the most hilarious joke of all time. But I still wish we could remember it. Maybe we'll hear it again in the drinking halls of Valhalla.

Memory is also how we learn anything. Even flatworms figure out, after a few bad experiences, to avoid the pathway with the electric shock. By contrast, it took me about four thousand trials to realize that drinking ultimately makes you feel *worse*. I was scandalized to learn that alcohol is technically a depressant. And once you've quit wiping your memory every night and having to reboot your whole personality every morning, your experience becomes cumulative instead of simply repetitive; you can start to see your life as something resembling a linear narrative, with an intelligible shape and possibly some meaning, instead of just a bunch of funny stories.

We couldn't go on living like that forever; as the traditional last call has it: "You don't have to go home, but you can't stay here." One by one my old drinking buddies succumbed to the usual tragedies: careers, marriages, mortgages, children. And as my own metabolism started to slow, the fun:hangover ratio became increasingly unacceptable. Eventually a day comes when the lined, puffy, sagging face you see the mirror when you're hung over does not go away, and you realize that it is now your actual face. The hangovers also acquired a dreadful new symptom of existential anxiety in addition to their more traditional attributes. Self-inflicted brain damage no longer seems so cool and defiant, nor wasting time so liberating. Squandering time is a luxury of profligate youth, when the years are to us as dollars are to billionaires. Doing the same thing in middle age just makes you nervous, not with vague puritan guilt but the more urgent worry that you're running out of time, a deadline you can feel in your cells.

I don't miss passing out sitting up with a drink in my hand, or having to be told how much fun I had, or feeling enervated and depressed for days. Being clearheaded is such a peculiar novelty it feels like some subtle, intriguing new designer drug. I don't know if it's one I'd want to get addicted to, though. After a week or so of feeling optimistic and silly, my energy level back up near 100 percent, I start getting antsy and bored. Apparently I'm not content to be happy. Sooner or later you want to celebrate your improved disposition with a cocktail.

I'm more productive now, and more successful; for the first time in my life I'm supporting myself by doing what I've always wanted to do. But I laugh less than I used to. Drinking was, among other things, an excellent excuse to devote eight or ten consecutive hours to sitting idly around having hilarious conversations with friends, than which I'm still not convinced there is any better possible use of our time on earth. Lately, in these more temperate years, I'm reminded of Shakespeare's Henry plays after Falstaff has died: Prince Hal, having spent his twenties as a drunken fuckup, puts riotous youth and disreputable friends behind and finds a place in life for dignity, honor, and achievement—but it also feels as if everything best and happiest and most human has gone out of the world. As if great things may lie ahead, but the good times are over.

Not long ago I celebrated my forty-second birthday. The evening started out grown-up and civilized, with Belgian ales and Chinese takeout at a quiet bar with friends, but the night took a turn for the puerile when one of my friends, whose age is the reverse of my own, insisted on taking me to another bar he knew nearby where patrons drink for free on their birthdays. This is the kind of bar I no longer spend any time in, having already logged eight hundred thousand hours in its like: a dark, raucous dive with cheap drafts and shots, loud rock and roll, and dank, graffitied bathrooms. He ordered me a concoction called a "car bomb," which, through some ingenious evil alchemy, is composed of three potent neurotoxins but tastes like a chocolate milk shake.  We punched Van Halen and Meat Loaf and the Charlie Daniels Band into the jukebox. We played fierce games of air hockey under a black light. We arm-wrestled with girls. Life was unbelievably great. It felt just like turning twenty-four. The next morning I was hung over, and forty-two.

The Czar's Daughter

The night we learned that our friend Skelly had unexpectedly died of a heart attack, his friends all got drunk in our respective cities and called one another back and forth throughout the rest of the night. A few hours after I'd phoned her with the news, Renée called me back from New Haven. "Tim," she said, in what sounded like all seriousness, "has anyone notified Skelly's daughter in France?" I could hear her husband, Kevin, laughing in the background.

There was no daughter in France, you see. A lot of the things our friend Skelly had told us about himself were not, in the strictest, most literal-minded sense of the word, true. Once, when our friend Lara was complaining that her older daughter had been telling lies, Skelly broke in to defend her. "She makes up stories," he protested. "She lies," Lara said flatly. Skelly, who knew better than to contradict Lara when she was in one of these moods, let it go with an eloquently equivocal expression, as if to say, *Well, that seems unduly harsh.* It was as though he could see no point in arguing with the kind of person who would denounce Santa Claus as a hoax. Obviously this is how he thought of what he did himself—telling stories, making a dull and mundane life a little more interesting for us all.

It would never have occurred to any of Skelly's friends to call him a liar. Despite his incidental falsehoods, he was a fundamentally genuine person. As his fellow fabulist Blanche DuBois once protested, "I never lied in my heart." He was authentic, decent, and kindhearted. Even though he was a very funny guy—ironic and self-deprecating, first to defuse an awkward moment with a dry aside—I can't remember hearing him ever once say anything funny at anyone else's expense, a statement I'm not sure is true of anyone else I've ever known. He'd had a younger sister with Down syndrome, and he told me he used to get in fights over her when he was a kid. He reproached anyone he heard using the middle school pejorative *retarded*. It was the only time I remember seeing him get angry, and we took it seriously, because it wasn't the anger of a chronically angry man, but of someone who was essentially gentle. All our friends' dogs recognized him as the nice one who always fed them and took them for walks. Rick and Lara's daughters inexplicably called him "Wally," a name that stuck. He told me that even as an adult he'd gotten into a few confrontations with people he saw mistreating animals or children. Whether this was literally true is irrelevant; the fact that he told such stories was a measure of his hatred of cruelty. Skelly's stories were expressions of his innermost self as pure and unconscious as dreams.

We met him while we were all working for one of those environmental groups that dispatch canvassers door-to-door to ask for contributions. The job was a refuge for people who were in what we'll call times of transition. If you were lucky, your transitional phase was just the normal postcollegiate drift, a breather in which to work a low-demand job and drink nightly while you tried to figure out What Next. If you were less lucky, it came after Life #1 had failed to work out. So there were, in addition to the hard-partying young people on staff, an older contingent of former salesmen, lapsed clergymen, aging hippies, empty-nest housewives, and recovering addicts. It was not initially clear to which of these groups Skelly belonged. His drinking and drug habits seemed to place him in the former group; he closed down the bars and smoked pot and crashed on couches and floors with the rest of us kids in our twenties. But it was hard to gauge how old he might be; he was evasive on that question, as on a number of others, and he had the preternaturally youthful look of a science fiction or fantasy writer, someone who'd never quite grown up. Our vague sense was that he was about ten years older than we were—that is, in his early thirties when we first met. But we were never sure of his real age until we saw the birthdate on his gravestone.

Gradually, in conversations in the van while we were waiting to be dropped off in suburban developments, or while having a smoke in neighborhood parks or playgrounds, putting off the dreaded moment of knocking on the first door of the evening, but mostly while sitting in the Rendezvous Lounge over cans of National Bohemian, an outline of Skelly's personal history emerged, almost all of it false. He had grown up in Baltimore, gone to a local college and law school, and practiced law for several years (verifiably true). He'd closed his practice a few years ago because he just hadn't enjoyed the work (qualifiedly true—it was a little more complicated than that). "When you're a lawyer, people call you up and tell you about their problems all day," he explained. "It's frankly not pleasant." He had lived in France for several years, and had a daughter there with a woman who'd died in a car accident; his daughter, Marie-Claire, was now in the care of her French grandparents, and he visited her once a year or so (totally untrue). He had just sold his first novel, titled *The Czar's Daughter,* to a New York publisher (I wouldn't bother looking for it on Amazon).

As we later explained it to ourselves, Skelly had told us his most blatant fabrications at the beginning of our acquaintance, in a job with a very high turnover rate, and he clearly hadn't expected to have to maintain these elaborate fictions for the next twenty years.

Eventually, depending on our individual levels of guilelessness, we realized that not everything he'd told us was factually accurate. I'm pretty guileless, as it turns out. I remember asking him once or twice when his novel was going to be published, which, thinking back on it, makes me cringe on behalf of us both. Our boss, Bianca, once saw him walking on Charles Street in Baltimore when he was supposedly visiting his daughter in France. After a while we stopped hearing anything about the novel, or the daughter, and we certainly didn't bring them up again. This is how it was with Skelly's stories: at first we actually believed them, then we pretended to believe them, and then we pretended we'd never heard them.

I was a cartoonist back then, and I used to incorporate caricatures of my friends into my drawings. I did this to Skelly only once—he was easy and fun to draw, with a mop of curly hair, a broad, froggy mouth, square glasses, and a mournful slope to his eyes that seemed to appeal to the viewer as if to say, *You see what I have to contend with?* In my cartoons, as in real life, he maintained an improbable dignity in the most demeaning of circumstances. But after his first appearance, Skelly forbade me ever to draw him again. At the time I thought he must just be sensitive about his appearance—and, admittedly, my caricatures didn't flatter anyone—but now I think there was more to it. I think it made him uncomfortable to know that he'd been observed. He once told me sagely, as though it were a personal motto: "The less people know about you, the better off you are."

We could dismiss Skelly's "stories," as we called them, easily enough by making affectionate fun of them behind his back. More persistent and worrisome were the things we didn't know about him, or weren't supposed to know. Like that he lived with his mother. If an older lady's voice ever happened to answer the phone when you called him, he explained, this was because if his phone rang a certain number of times the call was automatically forwarded to his mother's house. This was a feature I had never heard of the phone company offering. Rick started referring to the elderly woman who sometimes answered Skelly's phone as "the cleaning lady." It was years before any of us saw the inside of his house; Kevin, who was dropping him off one night, finally begged to use his bathroom. He later reported that the décor looked suspiciously unlike Skelly's taste: "I wouldn't've pegged Skel as a doily man." Eventually we all just discreetly dropped the pretense that he did not live with his mother without acknowledging that it had ever existed. By the time she died and we went to his house for the wake, where we met his mother's sisters and friends, it went without saying that she and Skelly had lived there together.

Another thing we weren't supposed to wonder about was why he was always broke. Kevin once said that Skelly was always twenty dollars short of having *exactly* the right amount of money. But none of us ever begrudged him a twenty or thought of him as a mooch. He'd make excuses about having already eaten when we'd go out to Sabatino's, the sprawling Italian eatery that was open till three, insisting he just wanted bread, but we'd always tell him to stop being silly and help himself to his share of the bookmaker's salad and order the tortellini. We were happy to pay for his company. We just liked it better when he was around. Now that he's gone, we occasionally burn a few hundred thousand bucks in Chinese Hell Money for him, figuring wherever he is he's probably already deeply in debt.

His destitution was understandable after he "cycled out" of (got fired from) the environmental canvass, during an interval of un- or underemployment. One night during this period I drove an hour and a half down Maryland's Eastern Shore to rescue him from a job working as a mate on an old sailing ship he'd nicknamed the *Nightmare,* which had broken down on its shakedown cruise and was in dry dock, where I found him hungry, freezing, and covered with epoxy. But it started making noticeably less sense after he started working at the Baltimore Opera's fund-raising office. You always had to triangulate the truth of Skelly's claims from the few available empirical clues, but we knew that he really did work at the opera (we'd seen his office and met his colleagues) and actually seemed to have risen to a position of some responsibility there. He was once sent to New York City for a training seminar for office managers, where he showed up with fifteen dollars in his wallet and no credit card, so that Rick had to put his hotel room on his own Visa, and also somehow lost his return train ticket, which I had to cover, and which he repaid with money he *wired* to me, necessitating a trip to one of those seedy check-cashing places down on Houston Street, where I had to stand in a long line of petulant, desolate people in a bare cinder-block room, plunging me briefly into the grim fiscal twilight world Skelly inhabited 24/7. "I have to work" became his standard excuse for not meeting you for a beer or showing up at a party. He seemed to do nothing but work, and yet somehow he was still always broke. It was something we talked and joked and wondered about, one of the Mysteries of Skelly, but somehow we never got any further than idle speculation over drinks. It turns out that when there is some conspicuous gap or contradiction at the center of someone's existence, there is probably a very specific, obvious reason for it, and the reason you're avoiding confronting it directly is that it's something you don't want to know.

For the last several years of his life, we weren't even certain that Skelly wasn't homeless. He seemed to spend a good deal of time at the library, and once told us a story about getting kicked out for falling asleep in the fiction department. One night when Kevin and I were in the city for a concert, we called Skelly up at the opera office because we were hoping to borrow twenty bucks' drinking money against the $∞.00 or so we'd loaned him over the years and also maybe crash at his house. He said, "Gee, I'm actually working late tonight, and I also have to get in early tomorrow, so I was just going to sleep on one of the couches here. But y'all are welcome to stay here, there's plenty of couches, they're surprisingly comfortable."

Kevin told him not to worry, never mind, we'd just drive home tonight—nah, we were sure, it was fine, we'd see him next time. He hung up and turned to me and said: "Skelly's lost the house."

He did seem to spend a lot of time either illicitly sleeping at his office or apartment-sitting for friends and coworkers. I often asked him why he didn't just sell his mother's house and use the money to rent a place in Mount Vernon, the midtown neighborhood where not only his workplace but the library and all the bars he frequented were located—where, essentially, he lived his whole life—and quit having to catch the last bus at 11 P.M. and ride forty minutes to the city limit to get home. He'd just shrug. I could only assume he was just too attached to the house where he'd grown up, where his mother had lived. I once loaned him a substantial amount of money so that the city wouldn't put a lien on the property. (One theory about where all his money went was that he was using it to pay off back taxes.) It wasn't until after he died that I realized that he couldn't have sold the house in the condition it was in, and, more important, that he could never have let anyone see the inside of it. I could only imagine, in retrospect, how cornered he must have felt when Kevin and I had called up asking to stay there, and I couldn't help but admire how coolly he'd thought on his feet.

It's hard to explain why we couldn't just come out and ask him, "Skelly, do you have a place to live?" It's not only because he wouldn't have told us; it just wasn't done. One of the more insidious properties of secrets is that they impose secrecy on the people around them, suborning them all into silence. In light of what we learned later, I wonder now whether we didn't, as they say in twelve-step programs, enable Skelly's habit. At first it was only out of common courtesy or discretion, an embarrassment for him, that we didn't challenge his stories. But in the end, as the things we knew we didn't know about him seemed stranger and more troubling and harder to ignore, it became a kind of complicity.

Occasionally, young women who learned that the things he'd

told them about himself weren't true felt betrayed. One of those girls, in a vindictive snit, actually snooped into his past and triumphantly spread the word about what she'd learned. I made a point of not hearing it. I knew that he really had been a lawyer at one time, although the only legal opinion I ever heard him offer, pro bono to Kevin and me over beers around three in the morning before our date to appear for a summons for illegal trespass, was: "I think y'all should blow off this court thing." ("Is that jurisprudential jargon, Skelly?" we asked him. "'Court thing'?") A woman I dated for a while, who'd gone to the same college as Skelly, asked around among her old classmates and found out that he'd been disbarred. I didn't stop her from asking, but I also told her I didn't want to know about it. I doubt whatever his transgression was would've shocked me—probably just drugs, or a minor and strictly temporary misallocation of funds, some petty and ill-concealed mischief. (Skelly had once explained to me, with the pleasure of a connoisseur of both language and human folly, the definition of the legal term *detour and frolic*.) But it would've felt like a betrayal of confidence for me to go behind his back and find out something about him that he clearly didn't want us to know. The fact that his lies had worked on those girls always seemed to me like a more telling indictment of them than of Skelly. They were angry because they'd been exposed as not just credulous but shallow; they'd been impressed by facts *about* Skelly instead of by him. And knowing things about someone is not the same as knowing him.

As far as I know, none of Skelly's friends cared about the facts of his life that embarrassed him so deeply. If anything, we were just sorry he'd ever felt the need to tell us these ridiculous stories. It implied that, on some level, he felt badly about himself, as if he didn't believe we'd like him for who he really was. What someone's lies reveal about them (aspirations to being an accomplished writer, fantasies of an exotic history and a cosmopolitan family) are always sadder than the fact of the lies themselves. These inventions illuminate the negative spaces of someone's self-image, their vanity and insecurities and most childish wishes, as we can infer from warped starlight the presence of a far vaster mass of dark matter.

Years ago a friend of mine and I used to frequent a market in Baltimore where we would eat oysters and drink Very Large Beers from 32-ounce Styrofoam cups. One of the regulars there had the worst toupee in the world, a comical little wig taped in place on the top of his head. Looking at this man and drinking our VLBs, we developed the concept of the Soul Toupee. Each of us has a Soul Toupee. The Soul Toupee is that thing about ourselves we are most deeply embarrassed by and like to think we have cunningly concealed from the world, but which is, in fact, pitifully obvious to everybody who knows us. Contemplating one's own Soul Toupee is not an exercise for the fainthearted. Most of the time other people don't even get why our Soul Toupee is any big deal or a cause of such evident deep shame to us but they can tell that it is because of our inept, transparent efforts to cover it up, which only call more attention to it and to our self-consciousness about it, and so they gently pretend not to notice it. Meanwhile we're standing there with our little rigid spongelike square of hair pasted on our heads thinking: *Heh—got 'em all fooled!*

What's so ironic and sad about this is that the very parts of ourselves that we're most ashamed of and eager to conceal are not only obvious to everyone but are also, quite often, the parts of us they love best. Skelly's stories themselves—not their content, but the fact of his telling them—were part of what we liked about him. Here's one of my very favorite Skelly stories: One Saturday Skelly was supposed to take a train up to my cabin to meet my friend Nick and me after work. Nick and I reluctantly left the deck overlooking the bay where we'd been eating oysters and drinking beers all afternoon and drove twenty-five minutes to meet Skelly at the train station. The train arrived: no Skelly. I checked my voice mail and found the following message (transcript verbatim from memory):

> *[Background noises of what is unmistakably the Mount Royal Tavern—loud conversation, raucous laughter, clinking of glasses, TV]*
> SKELLY: *Hey, guys, this is Skelly. Uh—I missed the train! I'm really sorry about this, but I was in a meeting that ran longer than I expected and—BLUUUUUUUUHRPP—I tried to catch it but I was, like, three minutes too late. So, I checked and there's another train at seven-twenty that gets in at seven-forty-five. I'll definitely be on that one, so hopefully y'all will get this message and be there to meet me. Um, okay, again, I'm sorry about that. I hope I'll see you soon.*
> *[Forty-five seconds of fumbling while Skelly tries to figure out how to hang up borrowed cell phone; continued bar noises in background]*

Nick and I had both been pretty peeved that we'd torn ourselves away from our pleasant setup on the water and driven half an hour down Route 40 to meet Skelly's train and he'd stood us up. But when I heard this message it became impossible to sustain any ill humor. I didn't even try to describe it to Nick; I just handed over the phone and let him replay it for himself. As he listened I saw his own annoyance deflate in the face of the sheer Skellyness of the message. It was amazing: no allusion to the aurally obvious setting of the call, no acknowledgment of the cartoonishly loud, elongated belch that interrupted his excuse. Sober, dignified, perfectly reasonable. Vintage Skelly. By the time he finally arrived we'd had another pitcher and replayed the message a half dozen times, finding it funnier and more incredible with each listening, slaying ourselves repeatedly. We greeted him more like a man returning from a moon landing or World Series victory than a guy who was an hour and a half late. Skelly seemed nonplussed. So he'd missed a train. What was the big joke? I'm quite sure we bought him dinner and beers.

There was something reassuring about Skelly's constancy—every time you saw him you remembered that no, you hadn't been exaggerating in recollection: he was *exactly* as you remembered, if not even more so. He was always broke, he always hit you up for a twenty ("forty would be even better, if you can spare it"), he was always the first to spill a beer, and he always happened to have that Led Zeppelin concert DVD along with him in case you were interested in maybe watching it on your computer later on. He was as dependably changeless as Wimpy from *Popeye* with his hamburger-on-credit habit. But that same quality also imposed a certain ceiling on our friendship. I became conscious, in those last couple of years, that there were certain boundaries I was never going to get past with him. I was always glad to see him, but we weren't getting any closer. And relationships have to grow to live. It was frustrating, but we all understood that you had to accept certain conditions with Skelly's friendship.

The only time I ever called him on his reflexive secrecy was once when we were having beers and I noticed that one of his fingers was swollen, black, and bandaged. "What the hell happened to your finger?" I asked. "Oh, you should've seen it a few weeks ago," he said, as though we were talking about a curious flowering plant or conjunction of planets. It emerged that he had developed a septic infection so serious he'd been hospitalized for a few days. He'd told no one—not his friends, not family. "Skelly," his friends tried to explain to him, "you gotta tell people if you're in the hospital. We want to know. People care about you." He just shrugged. "It was fine," he said. "I got to lay around and watch golf for a few days." We gave up in exasperation. *Fuckin' Skelly.*

He did tell me one thing in those last years that seemed touchingly revealing. Skelly had always had very troubled sleep—actually, "tortured" is more like it. He thrashed and snarled and pleaded with unseen persecutors. I think it may have been for his friends' benefit as much as his own that he cranked up the stereo whenever we all slept in the same space. What he told me was that sometimes, when he was trying to fall asleep, he would imagine himself buried under a pile of leaves, and tell himself: *They can never find me here.*

One weekend up at my cabin Nick and our friend Gabe, who both played in an informal semiweekly hootenanny in the back room of a South Baltimore bar, wrote a song about Skelly. It was kind of a mournful, stoic western number called "The Ballad of Tumbleweed Skel." The title was an allusion to his unpredictable appearances and abrupt and unexplained disappearances. You'd be drinking with him for hours and then at 11 P.M. or so you'd look around and say, "Hey, where's Skelly?" and he'd be gone—he'd have slipped off to catch his bus home without saying goodbye rather than face the inevitable gauntlet of peer pressure to not be silly and stay for just one more round. There were verses about his knowledge of Middle Earth arcana, his insistence on cranking up the Led Zeppelin when everyone else was trying to sleep, his terrible night terrors.

It wasn't 100 percent clear to me how Skelly, who had forbidden me ever to draw him, would react to this song if he heard it. But the next time he showed up at a hootenanny, months later, they busted it out unannounced. I wish you could've seen his face as he heard it—he was so abashed and flustered at finding himself the center of attention, but he was also helplessly grinning, laughing uproariously and clapping his hands at a good lyric, quickly recovering himself to catch the next one. It was like watching the face of the guest of honor at a celebrity roast, torn between chagrin and delight. I'm so glad he got to hear that song. He died less than a year later. It was our way of letting him know, in the most affectionately mocking way possible, *We've got your number.* And he loved it. Personal motto notwithstanding. For all his secrecy and his fear of being seen, he was touched that we had observed him so closely, and with such love. He loved that we knew him. This is

one reason people need to believe in God—because we want someone to know us, truly, all the way through, even the worst of us.

After Skelly died, a few of his best friends went through his house
to clean up before his extended family arrived. Suffice it to say we
learned what had tormented Skelly in his sleep. He had secretly
been mentally ill—or at least that's what we've been taught to call
it in the twenty-first century. You could also say, with as much real
understanding, that he had been plagued by demons. Even as he
had run his office and joked with his friends, at home, by himself,
he had ceased to live like a human being. He hadn't had electric-
ity or running water for a long time. The house was littered with
drug paraphernalia, but it was clear to us that the drugs were only
self-medication for the real problem. We also found objects whose
purpose—or meaning—we could not understand. We hauled
thirty-three large, industrial-strength bags of garbage out of that
house. After we'd stacked them all in a line in the back alley Kevin
said, "There," like an exasperated mom who's finally forced her
kid to clean his room. "Now was *that* so hard?" We all laughed,
a little hysterically. It had been an unspeakable day. When Kevin
and I had to go back in there after dark to check on one last thing,
we were frightened, like kids setting foot in a house known to be
haunted. We agreed that, if it hadn't been a row house, the thing
to do would've been to lob a Molotov cocktail in there and watch
the place burn.

I couldn't understand how he'd imagined no one would ever
find out about his secret life. He had simply had no long-term plan.
At some point he had stopped living as though he believed in a
future. Something seemed to have suddenly changed in the last
year and a half—that was around the time he'd stopped bothering
to open his mail or change his calendar. He'd assured me, about

a year before he died, that he'd just had a physical for work and they'd told him everything was fine. In retrospect, I can't believe that I believed this. Maybe I just wanted to let him give me a reassuring story so I could back off gracefully and let a touchy subject rest. But I wonder now whether he might not in fact have seen a doctor, perhaps when he was hospitalized for that infection, who told him something he didn't want to hear—a story whose ending he decided to rewrite.

In the first shock of discovery, I thought that Skelly had been a worse person than the one I thought I'd known. But now I think he was a better one. I've had other friends afflicted with huge, disfiguring secrets who ultimately revealed them. They integrated their secret selves into their normal lives, despite the pain and upheavals it caused. They freed themselves rather than let themselves be consumed. But Skelly was no less courageous, in a more inglorious way. He had to face more terrible monsters than most of us will ever have to know, and, in the end, he fought them to a draw. He kept them at bay, locked inside that house. *They can never find me here.* Like struggles to the death between submarine leviathans, it was a battle fought in utter darkness, invisible to the sight of the world. What tortures he suffered, and what unimaginable depths of bravery he summoned, are known only, if He exists, to God.

Skelly and I had had a sixteen-year-long running barroom argument over moral and metaphysical matters. He considered himself a Christian, albeit of an unorthodox, pot-smoking type. He always considered it a minor victory to get me to admit that we don't know why the universe is here instead of not, that this life is a mystery. After failing to convert me yet again he would affect to despair of my redemption and call me an "unabashed moral relativist" and we'd have another National Bohemian. I never said so, because I'm too polite (and because I imagine, like most atheists, that believers' faith is far more fragile than it is), but I always privately thought that religion was like one of Skelly's stories—an attempt to pretty up a cruddy and lusterless world. Skelly, like C. S. Lewis, thought the gospel was too strange, too unlikely, not to be true. It was simply too good a story.

He told me once, after reading an especially vituperative screed I'd written about the cruelty of the church or the cretinous bigotry of the Red States, that I was a better person than my beliefs. This is one of the things we rely on our friends for: to think better of us than we think of ourselves. It makes us feel better, but it also makes us be better; we try to be the person they believe we are. Skelly believed in his friends' best selves. It was another story he told—like most of his, better than the mottled truth. But it was also one of those magical stories, like those old science fiction tales about voyages to the moon, that make themselves come true.

In reciprocation of his generous suspension of disbelief on my behalf, I choose to believe that I did know Skelly, despite everything he dissembled and kept hidden. Of course we knew him. We spent hundreds—thousands—of days and long nights talking and drinking and eating with him and crashing on the same floors as the guy. He and I watched the sun come up over the ocean while silently trading sips from a bottle of whiskey in a hotel room in Atlantic City, with all our friends passed out around us. If that moment was not true, then nothing is. We knew his sanest, best, and, I would maintain, his truest self.

The worst part, for me, is imagining how alone he was. This is the most poisonous thing that secrets do to us—they isolate us from everyone around us and make us feel even lonelier than we already are. I wish he could've somehow brought himself to talk to us. I sometimes fantasize about how I would've reacted—what I would've said to him, how I would've tried to help. As Kevin once complained, "I wish he coulda just told us so we could've mocked him for it!" But not everybody gets to be free. Some have to stand guard at their own prisons for life. Some secrets we must take with us, as the melodramatic old idiom has it, to the grave.

And, after all, one never knew for sure. Once in a while one of Skelly's stories would be proven true and you'd be forced to question everything. For some perverse reason, anytime I flew anywhere I would always leave my car with Skelly. It spared him from having to use Baltimore's public transit system for a week or two, and it was pleasant to have him pick me up at the airport and stop off for a beer at the Midtown Yacht Club (not an actual yacht club). Once, when I got back from a trip, he gently broke the news to me over airport beers that my car no longer had a rear window. He explained that he'd just been driving it at a normal speed on Moravia Road when, suddenly and with no warning whatsoever, the rear window had simply fallen out and shattered into a million pieces on the pavement. I just nodded, understanding that I would never know the real story, whatever it may have been. I mentally wrote it off under cost-of-being-friends-with-Skelly expenses. Years later, driving that same car (window long since replaced), I was startled when, suddenly and with no warning whatsoever, the rear window simply fell out and shattered into a million pieces on the pavement. My immediate reaction, staring open-mouthed into my rearview mirror, was not *Hey my rear window just fell out* or *What am I supposed to do now?* but *Holy shit—Skelly was telling the truth!* I found this incident weirdly cheering. It not only vindicated Skelly but gave me a renewed sense of possibility in the world. Maybe there really was a daughter in France. Maybe Christianity was true! If the skies are ever rent asunder to reveal the archangel Michael raising his fiery sword to herald the return of Christ the King in all His glory, it'll be some consolation for me, before my damnation, to find Skelly among the Resurrected so I can buy him a beer and say, "We should've believed you."

When we die, all our secrets are loosed, like demons departing a body. Whatever subjective self we protected or kept hidden all our lives is gone; all that's left of us is stories. At Skelly's funeral, all his carefully guarded boundaries and compartments collapsed, and everyone he knew, the people he'd kept separate in life— family, friends, coworkers—all got drunk and commiserated and traded stories about him. I sat an ex-girlfriend of his down over shots of Irish whiskey and said, "Karin, I'd like to ask you a series of nosy questions." She smiled and said, "Go right ahead, Tim. I'd like to ask you some, too." It emerged over the course of our mutual interrogation that what I'd always assumed had been an on-again, off-again affair had been a platonic friendship. "He was a perfect gentleman," she told me, with a kind of defiant pride. His friends were bewildered to hear his employees describe him as *super*-organized, a perfectionist. "Wait, this is Skelly you're talking about?" we asked. "The guy who just died?" We retold the stories, as well-known and loved and ritualized in the telling as the Homeric epics or Icelandic sagas, about his walking off the pier in the fog, his getting arrested for trespassing on a submarine, the story of the Smallest Horse in the World. The legendarily clueless Bill Frug asked me the same question that Renée had the night we'd learned Skelly had died, but in all innocence: "Did anybody reach Skelly's daughter in France?" Incredibly, decades later, he still believed in her. It never occurred to me to disillusion him; it would've been like killing the last gryphon or chimera.

"No, Bill," I told him soberly. "We never found her."

The Parables of Skelly

The Felling of the Raiment.

14 Now a Dispute arose between the Four,
   And Discord was sown among them.
15 But The Lord smote Skelly's garment,
   So that it fell upon the Earth.
   And at once the Company was
   overcome with Mirth,
   And Lo, their Wrath was forgotten.

16 Now which of these men was truly
   naked?

-Gabe 7: 14-16

The Voice from Afar.

22 Skelly called unto them from afar,
   Saying He could not meet them,
   for He was about his Father's
   Business.
   But they could hear the clamor of
   the Tavern,
   And the Drink did betray Him.

23 Now tell me: Did Skelly speak truly?

-Nick 14:22-23

The Censer That Was Lost.

11 That night they trespassed,
   And did bathe in the Pool of
   a Neighbor,
   And fragrant herb was shared
   among them.
12 But in the morning the Neighbor
   found the Censer,
   And was sorely grieved, and did
   reproach them.

13 Skelly asked: Will the Neighbor
   return the Censer?

-Kevin 9:11-13

The Walking in the Water.

48 It came to pass that they were
   overcome with strong Drink,
   And took their rest upon a Landing.
   Skelly went alone unto the edge of
   the Water,
   And was lost to their sight in a Mist.
   And they heard a sound upon the Water
   As of a great Stone dropped into the Sea.
   And they cried out unto Him, saying:
   "Skelly? Where art Thou? Skelly?"

49 But He was no more among them.

- Alfie 17: 48-49

How They Tried to Fuck Me Over (But I Showed Them!)

I was a political cartoonist and essayist for the duration of the Bush presidency, so I was professionally furious every week for eight years. The pejorative *Bush-hater* always rankled me, presuming that my rightful outrage at that administration's abuses was as irrational as misogyny or arachnophobia. And yet, looking back at my own work from those years, even I am struck by its tone of shrill, unrelieved rancor. No wonder readers who met me in real life seemed pleasantly surprised to learn that I was so polite; they must've been expecting someone more like Ted Kaczynski or the guy from *Notes from Underground*. Reading over my own impassioned rants now, my impression is, *Jeez Louise, what a sorehead*.

A couple of years ago I realized something kind of embarrassing: anger feels good. Although we may consciously experience it as upsetting, somatically it's a lot like the initial rush of an opiate, a tingling warmth you feel on the insides of your elbows and wrists, in the back of your knees. Understanding that anger was a physical pleasure explained some of the perverse obstinacy with which my mind kept returning to it despite the fact that, intellectually, I knew it was pointless self-torture. It is, come to think of it, not unlike lust, which I also seek out insatiably, even though it subjects me to the sufferings of Tantalus.

Once I realized I enjoyed anger, I noticed how much time I spent experiencing it. If you're anything like me, you spend about 87 percent of your mental life winning imaginary arguments that are never actually going to take place. You make up little stories to explain misunderstandings and conflicts, starring yourself as innocent victim and casting your antagonist as a villain driven by sheer, unilateral, motiveless malice. If you've ever made the mistake of committing your half of these arguments to print or email, you probably learned, as I have, that the other person's half of the argument fails to conform to the script you wrote for them.

It seems like most of the fragments of conversation you overhear in public consist of rehearsals for or reenactments of just such speeches: shrill, injured litanies of injustice, affronts to common sense and basic human decency almost too grotesque to be borne: "And she does this shit *all the time*! I've just *had* it!" You don't even have to bother eavesdropping; just listen for that unmistakable high, whining tone of incredulous aggrievement. It sounds like we're all telling ourselves the same story over and over: How They Tried to Fuck Me Over, sometimes with the happy denouement: But *I Showed Them!* So many letters to the editor and comments on the Internet have this same tone of thrilled vindication: these are people who have been vigilantly on the lookout for something to be offended by, and found it.

We tend to make up these stories in the same circumstances in which people come up with conspiracy theories: ignorance and powerlessness. And they share the same flawed premise as most conspiracy theories: that the world is way more well planned and organized than it really is. They ascribe a malevolent intentionality to what is more likely simple ineptitude or neglect. Most people are just too self-absorbed, well-meaning, and lazy to bother orchestrating Machiavellian plans to slight or insult us. It's more often a boring, complicated story of wrong assumptions, miscommunication, bad administration, and cover-ups—people trying, and mostly failing, to do the right thing, hurting each other not because that's their intention but because it's impossible to avoid.

Obviously, some part of us loves feeling 1) right and 2) wronged. But outrage is like a lot of other things that feel good but, over time, devour us from the inside out. Except it's even more insidious than most vices because we don't even consciously acknowledge that it's a pleasure. We prefer to think of it as a disagreeable but fundamentally healthy reaction to negative stimuli, like pain or nausea, rather than admit that it's a shameful kick we eagerly indulge again and again, like compulsive masturbation.

And, as with all vices, vast and lucrative industries are ready to supply the necessary material. It sometimes seems as if most of the news consists of outrage porn, selected specifically to pander to our impulse to judge and punish, to get us off on righteous indignation. The more popular and lowest-common-denominator the media outlet, the more naked and shameless the appeal: think of tabloid headlines, wailing and jeering and all but calling for the public stoning of their indispensable scapegoats: accused killers, criminal billionaires, whichever foreign dictators are out of favor with the government. The morning of a blizzard in New York City, the *New York Post*'s headline was "ICE SCREAM: Fury as City Is Paralyzed by Blizzard." A subhead: "Outrage as Transit Stops in Its Tracks." My own impression of the blizzard was that it was pretty and fun, like a harmless, soft apocalypse. Walking around the city, I saw people trudging down the centers of empty avenues, children and grown-ups screaming with delight while sledding down hills in Central Park, a bar full of people in Santa suits getting drunk in the afternoon. But none of this qualifies as news, I suppose. PRETTY and FUN don't lend themselves to seventy-two-point headlines as well as FURY and OUTRAGE.

It's not just media specifically marketed toward the stupid that offer up this unwholesome diet, though they're the most overt about it. I used to drive around every day ranting back at the genteel NPR—snarling at Diane Rehm for fawning over that sexy old war criminal Henry Kissinger, or sputtering in rebuttal to some conservative flack who was arguing that it was naïve to expect the president to act as an "objective broker of information" (his euphemism for honesty). When I scan the daily headlines of prestigious publications like the *New York Times,* I'm semiconsciously seeking out stories that will provide fodder for the sadomasochistic pleasures of outrage and vindication, being wronged and proven right, *how-dare-you* and *I told-you-so.* Throughout the Bush years my very favorite story, the one I couldn't seem to read enough different iterations of, was "Republicans Ruining Everything"; a few months after Obama's inauguration it was "Republicans Still Writhing."

Any drug dealer knows it's bad business, and a fatal error, to start using your own product. I'm not immune to this stuff, even though I was a purveyor of it myself. I resisted the urge to draw any cartoons about fundamentalist Islam for years, less out of any PC sensibilities than for the same reason Bill Mauldin was loath to draw anti-Soviet cartoons: "I think of all the sons of bitches doing the same thing for reasons of their own and I usually throw the drawing away."[1] But in November 2007 the story of Gillian Gibbons, an English teacher in Sudan who was briefly jailed for allowing her students to name the class teddy bear Mohammed (a minor story in the mainstream press, but front-page news for a week in the tabloids), finally goaded me into drawing an absurdly blasphemous cartoon about other things being called Mohammed—a mixed drink, a hurricane, somebody's penis.

Afterward I was ashamed of my reaction, not because I'd offended anyone's religious sensibilities or been roused to xenophobic rage or made myself a tool of the imperialist propaganda machine, but simply because it had worked on me; I'd let myself be taken in, like any other rube. It was the same kind of mortified resentment you feel when you involuntarily tear up over a long-distance commercial or catch yourself rocking out to Cher or end up giving a dollar to a con artist whose hard-luck story is insultingly implausible. It was as if someone had activated an electrode in the outrage lobe of my brain. What was so disquieting was not just that I'd reacted with the programmed emotion, but that I'd believed I was genuinely feeling it.

It's risky to pursue these stories beyond the initial quick hit of anger, because it invariably turns out that the more you learn about them, the more disappointingly complicated and ambiguous and depressing they become. At one point I thought that a good use of my time would be to work myself into a rage over the mistaken shooting of the composer Anton Webern by an American GI at the end of World War II. There is no fetish so specialized that the Internet cannot gratify it; see the website "I Curse the Soldier Who Killed Anton Webern." But then I took my research a step too far and learned that the soldier who shot Webern, one Raymond Bell, was tortured by remorse for the rest of his short life. He died, an alcoholic, only ten years after the war. This story isn't morally satisfying at all. It's pointless and shitty and sad, a collision of victims. I'd been lured by a base craving into a finer, less comfortable feeling I hadn't expected or desired. It was like trying to seduce a girl and accidentally falling in love.

I'm not saying that we should all just calm down, that It's All Good. All is not good. There is plenty in any day's headlines to appall and infuriate any decent human being. The kind of piety that would have a schoolteacher whipped deserves to be mocked and vilified; my reasons for despising the Bush administration were sane and patriotic and moral. Outrage is healthy to the extent that it causes us to act against injustice, just as pain is when it causes us to avoid bodily harm. But pain can be perverted into masochism. And in my passionate *loathing* for the Taliban or the Bush administration, in my personal relationship to them, I'm really not much different from the kinds of housewives who used to write hate mail to the scheming villainesses on their favorite soap operas. The soaps refer to that character type, with dishy candor, as "the woman you love to hate"—one of the few contexts where you hear the love of hatred so frankly acknowledged. In political jargon, this sort of material is called "red meat," which is pretty contemptuously up-front about the nature of the beast whose appetite is being appeased. As David Foster Wallace asked in his essay on talk radio: "Aren't there parts of ourselves that are just better left unfed?"

One of the last news stories to elicit my uncritical outrage was the Somali pirate incident, a tense four-day-long drama in April 2009. Somali pirates seized an American cargo ship and held its captain hostage in a standoff with the U.S. Navy. What galled me was the presumptuous stance taken by the pirates that they, the maritime equivalent of a teen street gang, were negotiating from the same status as a legitimate nation-state. It only exasperated me further when the pirates' colleagues ("colleagues"—as if they were endocrinologists) vowed to take revenge on any Americans they captured in the future. They were criminals who'd gotten caught—shouldn't they be grateful we don't still hang pirates at the gibbet? I have to confess that it gave me some sanguinary satisfaction when the navy resolved the negotiations with snipers instead. It was one of the few news stories in recent memory that ended the way a TV movie would, not to mention the United States' first military victory in a decade.

My feel-good ending got annoyingly deflated when I saw the lone surviving Somali pirate brought in manacles to the United States, a place where he did not speak the language and knew not a soul. He was not exactly Blackbeard: in fact he looked a lot like a kid, which is what he was, and he was also inappropriately grinning a rather disarmingly goofy grin, as if he mistakenly thought he was up for a Golden Globe award. (In some cultures smiling is a cover for embarrassment or fright.) It's not as if he wasn't still a thug, or I suddenly felt like we ought to give the poor kid a break; I was just forced to notice he was a human being. I felt the same helpless gut empathy for him that I used to feel, unwelcome and against my better judgment, for George Bush in those moments when even he seemed to dimly apprehend that he was in way over his head. One reason we rush so quickly to the vulgar satisfactions of judgment, and love to revel in our righteous outrage, is that it spares us from the impotent pain of empathy, and the harder, messier work of understanding.

Grievances '08

THAT THING YOU LIKED?
THEY DON'T MAKE THAT ANYMORE.

TOTALLY GOT DE-FRIENDED,
MIDDLE-SCHOOL STYLE [1]

[1] THIS TURNED OUT TO BE SORT OF A MISUNDERSTANDING.

GOT IXNÆD FROM A PANEL
AT BIDDING OF FAMOUS COLLEAGUE [2]

THE FOOLS FAILED TO
APPRECIATE MY GENIUS

[2] ALSO A BIG MISUNDERSTANDING. HA, HA!
[3] NO IT WAS NOT ACTUALLY TOM WILSON, CREATOR OF ZIGGY.™

When They're Not Assholes

I never even learned the rules to most organized sports. I hid out in the art classroom during mandatory pep rallies and still avoid bars where a game is on because it scares me when people shout violently in unison at the TV. None of this helped much with my socialization as a male, but it has given me a certain outsider's perspective on the culture of sports. I noticed, when I was still very young, that during outcries over disputed calls, spectators' opinions about the play in question coincided, 100 percent of the time, with their team allegiance. As far as I could tell, no one was good-humoredly feigning their outrage for fun. They genuinely perceived the play to have gone the way that happened to favor their side. Instant replays did not modify these opinions. It's hard to imagine anybody saying, "Ahh, I don't know, actually it looked out to me," when all his pals are standing up from their bar stools yelling that it was in, the ref must be blind, it's a fix. He'd be like that four-eyed, bow-tied geek in the old animated cartoon cheering, "H'raay—I'm fer de udder team!" his vim shriveling as the entire crowd around him turns to regard him with surly hostility. The only times I've ever gotten emotionally invested in any sporting events were when a friend suckered me into rooting for the Buffalo Bills circa 1990–92, an experience that had the effect on me that campaigning for McGovern in '72 did on a generation of young voters, and once at a scripted jousting tournament in a Medieval Times theme restaurant, where, again, my fiefdom's champion lost ingloriously, this time to a prancing dandy called the Blue Knight. During my brief career as a fan I learned that the difference between actually believing something and just going along with the crowd is a lot less clear, more of a continuum, when you actually care about the game. And that caring has less to do with any real stake in the outcome than with having picked a side.

I endorse conservatives repealing health care reform in their own states, refusing to get flu shots for fear of government nanochips, carrying concealed weapons into bars. This is all just natural selection in action, elegant and just.

That was me, writing in the afterword to my last book of political cartoons. Perhaps you can tell I was overdue for a sabbatical. After eight years of pretending to be meaner and surer of myself than I really was, I found myself recalling the old parental warning to kids making grotesque or cruel expressions: "Your face will freeze that way." After Obama's inauguration, I spent a year or two detoxing from politics, keeping myself ignorant of current events like some nervous invalid who has to be protected from any news of the outside world lest he have one of his spells.

So when my friend Sarah, a cartoonist/journalist, asked me to accompany her to interview attendees at a Tea Party rally in front of the main post office in New York City on Tax Day, 2010, I saw it as an opportunity to venture back into the arena of politics and test out my tentative new policy of empathy and intellectual honesty. Even during my self-imposed information blackout I hadn't been able to avoid hearing about the Tea Party, a recrudescence of the far right sooner than I would've hoped. Depending on whom you ask, the Tea Party formed either as a spontaneous grassroots protest against the government's massive interventions in the economy after the financial collapse of 2008, an hysterical backlash against our first black president, or just a hasty rebranding of the Republican Party now that the name *Republican* had taken on the same stigma as the Pinto, DC-10, and other products that reliably self-destruct. Their platform was the usual Republican wish list—cut taxes, gut the government, repeal the last century and revoke the social contract—and happened to coincide with the financial interests of their billionaire backers. They were widely regarded, on the left,* as dingbats. But today I was going to resist the impulse to sneer and feel superior and instead try, for once, to listen.

What dooms our best efforts to cultivate empathy and compassion is always, of course, other people. At first glance, the crowd at the Tax Day rally unhelpfully confirmed all my snottiest liberal stereotypes about conservatives: beer bellies and mullets, cop mustaches and wraparound shades, baseball caps and star-spangled bandanas, Old Glory jackets and screaming eagle T-shirts, bad skin, fat asses, immobile helmets of hair. Most of the signs there were preprinted, for which I, a veteran of many a street protest, had the same low regard as I do for store-bought Halloween costumes. The printed signs were strictly on message—taxes, the budget, deficit spending—but, as at the antiwar rallies I attended back in 2002–2003, a lot of the hand-lettered slogans were ad hominem sentiments directed against the current president, many insinuating communist sympathies or even more sinister loyalties: the *O* in Obama rendered as a hammer and sickle, *Mao*bama,

---

*Throughout this essay I'm afraid I'll be using the terms *liberal, progressive,* and *the left* not quite interchangeably but pretty indistinctly, since they all now denote extinct or hypothetical entities rather than active political factions. *Liberal* is a term used almost exclusively by conservatives, and is loosely synonymous with *queerbait; progressives* are what liberals call themselves now that *liberal* is a slur (it's what *developmentally delayed* is to *retarded*); and as far as I can tell *leftists* are liberals who get mad if you call them liberals because liberals are all bourgeois patsies of The Man.

"Obama bin Lyin," etc. The MC proudly disclaimed the presence of any racists in the crowd, an assertion that seemed to be less for the benefit of the eavesdropping mainstream media (MSM) than for the crowd itself, which responded with defiant, self-congratulatory applause. (Should I mention that the only nonwhites I saw present were among a small contingent of NYU Young Republicans? I'm not interested in playing Who's the Racist here; what struck me as suspect was the complacent certainty that one is not a racist. Most of us liberals are so worried that we might secretly be racists that we're convinced this means we cannot really be racists.) A band played generic patriotic shitkicker rock. Someone nearly poked my eye out with the pointy gold finial on a miniature American flag (see illustration). I interceded in a rapidly escalating shoving match between a protester and a counterprotester, and got

to say the words "I'm sorry, ma'am, but your mom started it."

Inevitably, the crowd began chanting "U!S!A!" which has always seemed to me both scary and pathetic—scary because it feels as if it's pumping up some violent tension that can only be discharged by a book-burning or the ritual sacrifice of a foreigner—but pathetic because America is, after all, the most powerful military empire in the history of the planet; we spend the equivalent of most countries' GNP each year maintaining an armada of battleships the size of cities, a fleet of radar-invisible supersonic bombers, and enough nuclear weapons to denude the entire biosphere of the earth, and still we need to *root* for ourselves? It reminds me of the kinds of feeble egos who need to invest themselves in boringly infallible sports franchises like the Yankees, who can afford to buy the championship year after year. I've always felt that the guys in America chanting *U!S!A!* and the guys in the Middle East chanting *Death to America!* had way more in common with each other than either of them did with me. At one antiwar protest, I remember, a counterprotester challenged us all, from across a police barricade, to chant "U!S!A!" along with him. We kinda tried, but it sounded stiff and timid and trailed off pretty quickly. "See, you can't do it!" he exulted, as if he'd outed us all as vampires by waggling a Bible at us. I think we were less embarrassed by our halfhearted chanting than by the fact that we'd let ourselves be bullied into trying in the first place.

My friend Lauren and I used to carry a casket-sized American flag at antiwar marches, and I wore a flag lapel pin at my cartoon readings during the War on Terror, but it was like when porn models dress as "nerdy girls" by putting on a pair of glasses and holding a prop book; you can appropriate the accessories, but the gestalt is all wrong. Somehow I felt like an impostor at the Tea Party rally when it came time to sing the national anthem; even though I've been known to play a swelling rendition of "The Star-Spangled Banner" on my own foot-pedal pump organ, in this context I felt inhibited singing along, like an uptight Mennonite nervously mouthing the words to a familiar hymn in a church full of charismatic Baptists all sobbing and ululating and toppling white-eyed all around him. In this crowd, it felt like the anthem of a different country, one in which I was an alien.

I was uncomfortably aware of a subtle checking of identity papers here. People kept giving Sarah and me wary looks and asking us who were "with." Partly this was because Sarah was interviewing people with a digital recorder, and they suspected us of being stooges of the MSM, but it also had to do with our dress and de-meanor. It was the same look I used to get every time I ever walked into a rural Maryland dive bar: all heads would turn my way and give me a dubious once-over, as if to say: "The fuck *you* doin' here?" For the Tea Party rally I had costumed myself in a double-breasted suit with a pocket square and gold-rimmed glasses. This was a miscalculation. I had dressed as a Wall Street Republican; these were the Wal-Mart Republicans.

"He looks like a Moby to me," said the lady I'd prevented from beating someone up, well within earshot and staring right at me.

I cupped an ear at her. "A what?" I said.

"A Moby," said her daughter.

"I don't know what that is," I said.

"Well 'at's yer problem, idn'n it?" she snapped.

"That woman said I looked like a Moby," I told Sarah.

"A 'Moby'?" she said. "Like the musician?" She looked at me, puzzled. "You have much more hair."*

I was starting to remember the whole problem now: I hate these fucking people. It's never been just political; it's personal. I'm not convinced anyone in this country except the kinds of weenies who thought student council was important really cares about large ver-sus small government or strict constructionalism versus judicial ac-tivism. The ostensible issues are just code words in an ugly snarl of class resentment, anti-intellectualism, old-school snobbery, racism, and who knows what all else—grudges left over from the Civil War, the sixties, gym class. The Tea Party likes to cite a poll show-

---

* A "Moby" is defined by urbandictionary.com as "an insidious and specialized type of left-wing troll who visits blogs and impersonates a conservative for the purpose of either spreading false rumors intended to sow dissension among conservative voters, or who purposely posts inflammatory and offensive comments for the purpose of discrediting the blog in question." (It is in fact etymologically derived from the name of the musician, who advocated the tactic in an interview.) Looking this up later made me feel it was just as well that I hadn't followed through on that morning's impulse to paint a sign saying "KILL THE HIPPIES."

ing that their members are wealthier and better educated than the general populace,[1] but to me they mostly looked like the same people I'd had to listen to in countless dive bars railing against "edjumicated idiots" and explaining exactly how Nostradamus predicted 9/11, the very people I and everyone I know fled our hometowns to get away from. So far all my interactions at the rally were only reinforcing my private theory—I suppose you might call it a prejudice—that liberals are the ones who went to college, moved to the nearest city where no one would call them a fag, and now only go back for holidays; conservatives are the ones who married their high school girlfriends, bought houses in their hometowns, and kept going to church and giving a shit who won the homecoming game. It's the divide between the Got Out and the Stayed Put. This theory also accounts for the different reactions of these two camps when the opposition party takes power, raising the specter of either fascist or socialist tyranny: the Got Outs always fantasize about fleeing the country for someplace more civilized—Canada, France, New Zealand; the Stayed Put just dig further in, hunkering down in compounds, buying up canned goods and ammo.

But, see, I'm doing it again. This is the craft I practiced during the Bush years: polemic, invective, and caricature. It's just so easy and fun. It's also automatic—a defense against people who all seem to hate you for no reason. Yes, I know how it makes me sound. And I can imagine what the people at the Tea Party rally must've seen when they looked at me: some overdressed, arrogant, East Coast ivory-tower Pellegrino-sipping liberal elitist who probably regards them as too ignorant, misinformed, or just plain stupid to have the right to an opinion, much less a vote, and who'd come here just to judge and make fun of them—all of which is, to be fair, completely accurate.

Actually one lady did compliment my tie. I'd almost forgotten her. See, to make all these fun unfair generalizations I'm conveniently airbrushing out the exceptions in the crowd, like Delia, a member of the NYU College Republicans who shyly asked me about the book I was carrying. I showed her David Lipsky's interview with David Foster Wallace, a writer she hadn't heard of, and got to feel politely patronizing until I asked her what she was reading—which proved, to my unfeigned astonishment, to be Mervyn Peake's *Gormenghast* trilogy. Delia was an econ major, and she was here, she explained, because she was opposed in principle to Keynesian economics. I made a mental note to look up Keynes later on and asked her, in the most tactful and roundabout way, so as to avoid the potential implication that she was a warmonger or a racist or anything: so, um, but then why protest now and not over the previous eight years, when Bush was bankrupting the country by starting two wars while cutting taxes? Hadn't that been the fiscal equivalent of buying a vacation house and a powerboat at the same time you quit your day job? She informed me that the annual budget deficit had increased by nine times in the year that Obama had been in office, and that under his new budget the national debt would triple by 2019.* I said, "I did not know that." This datum basically passed through my brain as a neutrino does through the earth, interacting with nothing. If I tried to account for these horrific expenditures at all, I figured they were probably necessary to salvage the economy from the shambles in which the Bush administration had left it. This is called "the confirmation bias"—retaining information that supports your preconceptions and forgetting anything that contradicts them. It was like seeing an instant replay showing that your team's hit was out.

Still, I had to wonder whether Delia felt at ease in this crowd,

---

* As with a lot of these figures, it depends on how you calculate it. According to the Congressional Budget Office, Delia's claims are essentially correct, although it's also true that when Obama took office he inherited a deficit of about $1.2 trillion, so it's not like this is all the result of typical liberal tax-'n'-spend policies run amok. (All information from CNN Factcheck, January 30, 2010.) Actually getting to the bottom of these factoids is so boring and hard to follow—especially for someone like me who's not clear on the difference between annual deficits and the national debt or what the economy even *is,* exactly—that it's no wonder most of us just stick to reciting whichever talking points support our side.

most of whom probably had less vehement opinions about Keynes versus Hayek than about Ford versus Chevy. But then anytime you join in a mass movement you're going to find yourself standing alongside idiots. One reason people go to mass rallies is to become stupider and surer of themselves than they are when they're alone. I saw plenty of people at antiwar protests I wouldn't have wanted to talk to at a party: the well-meaning Wiccan who told my friend Lauren and me it was good to see some "normals" there, the guy who sneered, "Why are you carrying *that*?" at the American flag we were holding, or the Eminem wannabe atop a flatbed truck draped with Palestinian flags who kept bellowing hoarsely over a loudspeaker, "WHAT DO WE WANT?" to which we were supposed to respond, in bellicose unison, "PEACE!" Not to mention the inevitable contingent of hippies urging us to LEGALIZE HEMP or at the very least to SMOKE WEED, who seemed to believe that their giant puppets and drum circles would cause karmic tremors in the corridors of power.

One of the things I felt at the Tea Party rally was envy, the complicated kind a divorcée might feel at a wedding, or an atheist at a baptism. I remembered how romantic and fun it was to stand up against a monolithic power, side by side with people you loved, for something you believed in. You got to feel courageous, besieged, and undeniably in the right. And even though I don't endorse their agenda, I'm not wholly unsympathetic to the Tea Party's grievances. I, too, increasingly feel as if paying my taxes is like giving money to a junkie—I know it's all going straight into the arm of investment banks and Afghanistan. I might've liked to see executives at Goldman Sachs paraded down Wall Street in pickup truck tumbrels rather than lavishly rewarded with more of my money. And most of the people who've joined the Tea Party feel these injustices much more personally than I do. They understand that nobody in power gives a shit about them anymore. They watched Bush and then Obama bail out the authors of the financial crisis instead of its casualties. They see economic recovery measured by the Dow Jones and Nasdaq instead of the minimum wage or the price of milk. Also, even though many of them would punch you in the face if you were to suggest that America is any # other than 1, I'm sure they feel as clearly as I do that sick, vertiginous lift in their guts when you're in something very large that's starting to fall. All their apocalyptic rhetoric about a socialist takeover isn't just panic at the imminent prospect of an America that's no longer majority white; it's a distorted recognition that ours is a nation in decline. And they probably see more clearly than I do that the fates of Red and Blue America are not intertwined, but increasingly divergent. The so-called "creative class" is manning vital industries like social marketing, graphic design, and creative nonfiction, while those peons back in flyover country who used to make quaint passé trinkets like steel are SOL.* It seems likely that in the future the coastal cities will resemble post-imperial nations like France— pleasant places to live with world-class museums and restaurants as souvenirs of their brief time at the top—while the heartland is already starting to look more like post-Soviet Russia, with crystal meth instead of vodka. They know that we've cut them loose. That they're expendable.

At this point the Tea Party and progressives have more in common with each other than either of us does with moderates: at least we're passionately engaged citizens instead of dull-eyed consumers, and we're both ideological purists who aren't pushing for reforms so much as a razing of the status quo. The main difference between us is in our preferred villains: the left blames Corporate America for the ruinous state of the union, while the right blames the Government. Not many people on either side seem to have noticed that these alleged antagonists are literally the same people. They move from regulatory agencies to lobbying firms, Congress

---

*Department of Labor classification for "Shit Out of Luck."

to corporate boards and back like Afghani warlords switching sides between Coalition and Insurgency depending on who's paying better that week.

Watching middle-class conservatives vote for politicians who've proudly pledged to screw them and their children over fills me with the same exasperated contempt I feel for rabbits who zigzag wildly back and forth in front of my tires instead of just getting off the goddamn road. You'd think that given our shared loathing for the Wall/K Street oligarchy that's running this country like a Ponzi scheme we'd be able to put aside our brand loyalties, achieve what Hungarian Marxist György Lukács called "class consciousness," and finally form that formidable coalition the American political philosopher Charles Daniels called "the cowboys and the hippies, the rebels and the yanks."[2] But even if you could convince the people at the Tax Day rally that our common interest lay in publicly funded elections or revoking corporations' legal status as individuals, you'd still never get them to work alongside progressives, because when they look at us they see a bunch of electively unemployed anarchists with blond dreadlocks, fashionable disfigurements, and tribal tattoos appropriated from peoples their own ancestors exterminated. And good luck persuading me to repeal the income tax or eliminate the Federal Reserve or that this crowd has the answer to anything at all. We are just not each other's kinds of people.

What exactly these two kinds of people are is a question that's been the subject of a lot of dubious ideation over the last decade or so. One study at the University of California at Berkeley collated the results of fifty years' worth of psychological research literature and correlated conservatism to a constellation of personality traits like authoritarianism, dogmatism, intolerance of ambiguity, the need

for cognitive closure, and something called "terror management."
It concluded: "the core ideology of conservatism stresses resistance
to change and justification of inequality,"[3] which even I can't help
but notice is a pretty judgmentally loaded way of putting it. (You
could also say "ensuring social stability and rewarding merit.")
These findings seem to be corroborated by neuroscience: a recent
study of brain scans[4] reveals that in conservatives the amygdala,
a structure associated with fear, is enlarged, while in liberals, the
anterior cingulate cortex, which is concerned with detecting errors,
monitoring conflict and uncertainty, and empathy, is more highly
developed—all of which is presumably why Republicans like elec-
trocuting criminals and bombing foreigners and we lefties are such
dithery, ineffectual do-gooders.

I find these studies really appealing for reasons that make
me uncomfortable. Regardless of their scientific merits, which
I'm not qualified to judge, they're just as reassuring and self-
congratulatory as my own theory about the Got Out versus the
Stayed Put. They remind me faintly of all that nineteenth-century
phrenological research that purported to prove that Negroes were
an evolutionary stage between Europeans and apes. Psychologists,
sociologists, philosophers, and other eggheaded academics tend to
be overwhelmingly liberal, so it is perhaps suspect that they'd try
to pathologize—or at least reduce to psychological symptoms—
a perfectly legitimate and widely shared political ideology. What
interests me more than any of these theories is the need to formu-
late such theories—to establish some basic, empirical distinction
between these two groups, like the evolutionary split between the
Eloi and the Morlocks, a difference not of opinion but of kind.

The truth is, there are not two kinds of people. There's only one:
the kind that loves to divide up into gangs who hate each other's
guts. Both conservatives and liberals agree among themselves, on
their respective message boards, in uncannily identical language,
that their opponents lack any self-awareness or empathy, the abil-

ity to see the other side of an argument or to laugh at themselves. Which would seem to suggest that they're both correct. I like to believe that liberals are the ones who are at least trying to transcend this sort of tribalism, who Celebrate Diversity and promote tolerance and think of themselves as citizens of the world instead of parochial nationalists, which is what makes us such bad chanters, but I have to admit that our contempt for those primitive, tribal conservatives is itself pretty tribalistic.

This cultural divide serves all kinds of powerful interests: the *Tom & Jerry*–level narratives required by the infotainment industry, the vampiric longevity of a two-party system that last represented any actual constituents around the time I learned to color inside the lines, and, above all, the portfolios of the obscenely wealthy, for whom it serves as a convenient diversion while they help themselves to the last of the money. But it's not as if anyone needed to invent it. Maintaining any sort of dogmatic ideology necessarily involves some exhausting intellectual dishonesty—forcibly ignoring dissonant information, dismissing counterarguments, constantly reassuring yourself that you're in the right—and seeing what we've repressed in ourselves unapologetically embodied in someone else infuriates us. Immediately after 9/11, I was secretly relieved that we had heartless warmongering bastards like Dick Cheney in the White House, because I knew they would wreak some suitably Valhallan vengeance. It was only when I saw crowds of crew-cut frat boys chanting "U!S!A!" with open red mouths, and slogans like FUCK ISLAM scrawled on the sides of cardboard missiles, that I recoiled from my own ugly bloodlust. It was like seeing some dick in a shopping mall who turns out to be you in a mirror. I realized that where I belonged, on any given issue, was on the opposite side of a police barricade from those guys. Red and Blue bash each other with the hysterical homophobia of the closeted because we recognize in each other our most loathed secret selves. We're the Red States' feckless, ineffectual, faggy compassionate side that they like to think they've successfully quashed, just as they, those angry chanting bandanaed rednecks, are our more credulous and aggressive selves, whom we're too inhibited to own up to. Thus conservatives have coined pejoratives for compassion and altruism—"bleeding heart," "do-gooder"—while liberals get nervous and ironic in the presence of passionate patriotism and religious zeal—what we call "flag waving" and "Bible thumping." We are one another's political Shadows. We may hate each other, but let's at least quit pretending we *hate* hating each other; we love hating each other.

I'm afraid most people choose political parties based on the same question they ask about regular parties: *Who else is going to be there?* Even though the facts in the debate over the invasion of Iraq were few and unclear when they weren't deliberate fabrications, I had no difficulty figuring out where I belonged: look, lined up over on that side, all the guys who ever called me a faggot in high school or beat me up outside a bar, all chanting "U!S!A!"; on the other, my friends and all the hot girls. When I listened to Tony Blair's defense of the invasion of Iraq, I was abashed to realize that if we'd had a president who'd been half as eloquent, and had flattered my intelligence instead of appealing to fear, I might well have been persuaded to support the war. It turns out I respond to the Pavlovian stimulus of propaganda as reliably as the next rube—Bush was just using the wrong brand on me. (I'm essentially no different from those ignorant schlubs who cast their vote for the candidate they'd rather have a beer with—I'd just rather have beer with a different kind of guy.) I disagreed with Christopher Hitchens's advocacy of the Iraq War, but I couldn't help but admire his integrity—or maybe it was just cussedness—in breaking ranks with his own ideological allies, risking the scorn and moral opprobrium of his former friends and allying himself with people he must have despised. But it troubles me to see how rarely this happens.

You'll blunder up against these unspoken taboos if you venture a heterodox opinion or just mention a fact that clashes with your side's official narrative. For example: for all its crimes and ineptitude, the Bush administration tripled the amount of money funneled into humanitarian aid and development in Africa, and did more to combat AIDS in sub-Saharan Africa than the previous Democratic administration. The name George Bush still drops out of my friends' mouths like something that wasn't supposed to be in their food, but it's evidently spoken with respect in places like Sudan. When I mentioned this to some friends over beers, it kinda clunked awkwardly onto the table. Nobody knew what to do with it. "Well," they'd allow grudgingly, "at least they did one thing right." Or they'd float the notion that they'd done it for cynical reasons, to compete with Chinese influence in Africa, or that some underling in the administration had done it without any higher-ups' knowledge. It came as a real relief when someone speculated plausibly that it must've been a giveaway to a pharmaceutical company. It still felt impolitic, almost treacherous, of me to have mentioned it. As a friend of mine once sighed: "I hate it when they're not assholes."

Which is kind of how I felt when I ran into someone I knew at the Tea Party rally. It was one of those out-of-context moments where, for a few seconds, you can't recognize someone you know you've seen many times because they're not where you usually see them: the bodega clerk in a bar, your therapist at the Y.

"Matt?" I said, experimentally.

It *was* Matt. He was a former student of mine, from a cartooning class I'd taught. Now that I recognized him, it made perfect sense that Matt would be here. Matt was an aspiring political cartoonist with rightward-leaning libertarian sensibilities, working under the nom de plume "Slim Dodger." I'd laughed out loud at a portrait he'd painted of Obama wearing the big frowsy gray beard of Karl Marx, captioned GROW A BEARD—SOCIALISM'S HERE! because it turns out anybody looks hilarious in a Karl Marx beard, but especially Barack Obama, his grin splitting through the nimbus of whiskers. It wasn't my job as his instructor to argue with Matt's characterization of Obama as a socialist. My main criticism of that cartoon was to caution him against its looking like an uncharacteristically merry Frederick Douglass.

"So are you writing about this," Matt asked me, "or . . . ?"

"Um, I'm not sure yet," I said. Which was true, and yet I felt myself squirming a little. Matt certainly knew my own political sensibilities from my work, and he must've known that I was not there as a wholly sympathetic observer. I noticed he was wearing a yellow T-shirt with the word MARSHAL across the chest. I suffered an irrational spasm of worry that he might identify me as a liberal infiltrator and I'd be thrown out or torn to pieces by the mob, an infidel at Mecca, but of course no such thing happened. He told me he'd gotten involved with the Tea Party only a few months before, but it was such a loose, grassroots structure that within a couple of weeks he'd found himself in the role of organizer. We chatted for a few minutes more before he had to resume his duties and Sarah and I fled to debrief over beers.

A few weeks later I saw Matt profiled in an article on the New York City Tea Party in one of the city's alternative weeklies, and sent him a note of congratulations. There's a conspicuous lack of any talented political cartoonists on the right, and it occurred to me that if Matt were to become a successful conservative cartoonist I'd be perversely proud to tell people I'd been one of his mentors. Even old Obi Wan Kenobi, seeing his former student now some sort of big shot on the Death Star with legions of stormtroopers scuttling around at his command, must've thought: *The kid made good.* The student/teacher relationship supersedes ideological differences, which is as it should be. I've seen so many friends and families sundered and turned against each other by politics. I know people who've been disowned because they're atheists or bisexual, people who love their parents painfully but can't even talk to them about the news without getting into a tearful shouting match. To me this seems not just sad but obscene, like a symphony interrupted by a ringtone. Let me propose that if your beliefs or convictions matter more to you than people—if they require you to act as though you were a worse person than you are—you may have lost perspective. Over Belgian ales Sarah remembered an Israeli friend of hers who'd reminded her, when a conversation about the Situation had come to a sputtering impasse, "You know, we don't have to agree about this." Perhaps in a country where political struggles involve suicide bombings, military incursions, and actual fortified concrete walls it's easier to keep mere differences of opinion in perspective. In America, where we've endured exactly two days of foreign assault on our soil in the last century and now use words like *warfare* to refer to progressive taxation, we've made partisan loyalty a precondition of friendship, and escalated our wonky policy squabbles into an hysterical internecine war.

I'm not issuing some naïve plea for civility or bipartisanship here, or pretending that the opposing sides in this fight are intellectually equal. We have irreconcilable visions of the kind of country we want this to be: some of us would just like to live in Canada with better weather; others want something more like Iran with Jesus. My cruelest hope for the Tea Party is that one of their candidates wins the nomination for the presidency and they implode of their own hubristic stupidity. But at least when I hear about them now, instead of reflexively picturing some braying ignoramus like Michele Bachmann, I try to remember that Matt's out in that crowd somewhere, too. God agreed to spare Sodom if ten good men could be found within its walls (Abraham had to haggle him down from fifty). He ended up napalming those perverts anyway but the basic principle of sparing the sinner for the sake of the righteous, or the shithead for the sake of the basically okay, remains sound. As Sarah's Israeli friend pointed out, Matt and I don't have to agree. It can't have been easy for him to be a conservative at a Manhattan

art school; he told me he'd "graduated persona non grata" after
outing himself in that article. In his interview he mentioned that
his parents had been small business owners, and he remembered
listening to Rush Limbaugh in the car with his mother. I came by
my own indefensible utopian notions not from studying political
science or history but from having pacifist parents, reading science
fiction, and watching a lot of *M*A*S*H*. Matt's ideology, like mine,
has less to do with what he thinks than whom he loves. Which is
one reason why any attempt at a "national conversation" degener-
ates almost immediately into a shoving match. *Your mom started it.*

America will never be either Canada or Iran. It's far too sprawling
and motley, barbaric and hilarious. Any generalization you try to
make about politics will unavoidably be bullshit in a country that
includes Truthers, Birthers, Flat Earthers, Earth Firsters, militant
vegans, and Christian swingers, people who believe the government is controlled by the Illuminati, George Soros, or extraterres-
trial reptiles. This nation was founded by wackos who were driven
out of their homelands over their subversive politics and lunatic
religions, and a nation of wackos we remain. Like absolutely everyone else in America, including people currently in bunkers
awaiting the onslaught of the Islamofascist fifth column, I don't
think of myself as an extremist, or even especially political, just as
a guy who believes in common sense and human decency trying to
live in a country gone bonkers. I, too, am a wacko.

I have a neighbor at my cabin on the Chesapeake Bay who's a
former marine and a Republican. We're both eccentric artists and
middle-aged bachelors who are disturbingly overinvested in our
pets. He keeps an eye on my cat for me when I'm out of town and
complains about her bitchy ingratitude; I sent him a hand-drawn
sympathy card when his detestable potbellied pig died. I do have to

set firm limits on my involvement with his various moneymaking schemes—the department store custom-engraving gig, the gourmet potato chip franchise, the TV pilot script about the blind hit man. He and I inhabit almost wholly separate informational universes: he watches Fox and listens to a lot of talk radio; I read the *Times* and listen to NPR. We don't just disagree about political issues; we haven't even heard about the news stories each other is incensed about. My ex-girlfriend Margot once got into it with him over Ronald Reagan while drinking whiskey around a bonfire and things got uncomfortable fast, but, because we're neighbors, he and I mostly don't talk about such things. His only comment after reading my collection of scabrous cartoons about the Bush administration, offered after a judicious pause, was: "Well—some of us have to be right, and some of us have to be wrong." We both laughed. Once in a while he invites me up to his house for what he calls a "martini," by which he means a gigantic tumbler filled with pure rail vodka and garnished with whatever pickled vegetables he has in the fridge—cocktail onions, okra, tomatillos. We'll carefully clunk glasses and say "Cheers," and then I suddenly wake up the next morning with my skull thumping and miasmic memories of having a second "martini," whomping down a huge pepper-encrusted steak, and, improbably, of my neighbor and me watching old video footage of Brian Wilson and Freddie Mercury in concert, both of us getting all weepy. I'm pretty sure that he and I describe each other behind each other's backs in much the same terms: "Oh, he's definitely a nutjob, but you gotta love the guy." In this, I believe, there is hope for America.

The Anti-Kreider Club

Yesterday my friend Harold reported another Felix sighting. Harold was walking out of a supermarket in Baltimore when he happened to see Felix walking in. Felix made a gesture of casual command at the automatic doors and a sound effect under his breath like *mmwOWm*, which Harold understood was meant to indicate that Felix was opening the door *with his mind*. My laughter at this story was fond and grudging, the kind that says: *That fuckin' guy.*

I haven't seen Felix in over ten years. We met on the first day of fourth grade, in 1976, when we were nine years old. Grown-ups aren't supposed to talk about "best friends," but he was among my closest and certainly my most constant friend from then until we were well into our thirties, when he inexplicably disappeared on me. I don't mean he fled the country or changed his identity or got abducted; the last I heard he was still living in Baltimore. He just stopped returning my calls. It took me almost a year of leaving messages on his answering machine to get the hint. It took me much longer to understand that I was never going to know what had happened.

Losing a friend may not hurt as intensely as a romantic breakup, but it often hurts more deeply, and for longer. I can have friendly and affectionate exchanges with women over whom I was publicly sobbing just a few years ago, but being reminded of Felix, whom I haven't seen or spoken to for over a decade, still makes me go quiet with puzzlement and sadness. Society doesn't officially recognize friendship as an institution in the way it recognizes sexual relationships, so there's no real protocol for ending one. If you've been going out, dating, or just sleeping with someone for even a month or two and you want to stop seeing him, you're expected to have a conversation with him letting him know it and giving him some bogus explanation. This conversation is seldom pleasant, and it ranges in tone from brittle adult discussions in coffee shops to armed standoffs in day care centers, but once it's over, you at least know your status.

Because there's no formal etiquette for ending a friendship, most people do it in the laziest, most passive and painless way possible, by unilaterally dropping any effort to sustain it and letting the other person figure it out for themselves. (I do know some people who've explicitly renegotiated the boundaries and conditions of friendships—saying *From now on we don't talk about my personal life*, or *Listen, I can't be your confidante anymore*—but these people have all been female. I hesitate to draw any broad generalizations along gender lines, but it feels to me as if it's a taboo, in male friendships, to talk about the friendship itself.) When I've had to end friendships myself, I've been just as graceless and craven about it. Listening to the other person's puzzled phone messages, reading their jokey/plaintive texts ("ARE U ALIVE?"), I feel the same way I do when I smack an insect and it doesn't quite die but lies there piteously writhing. When it's you doing the defriending, the defriendee seems needy and obtuse, not getting the obvious message, overstepping the boundaries everyone else understands implicitly. You want to say: *Look: we were friends* in college. *That was twenty years ago.* It's always you who's the reasonable one, and the other who's being either unfathomably cruel by defriending you or clingy and demanding by not accepting their defriending with dignity.

I should clarify that this method is painless only for the de-
friender; for the defriendee it's more like getting buried in sand
up to your neck and left for the ants. Because the end of a friendship isn't even formally acknowledged—no Little Talk, no papers
served—you walk around effectively heartbroken but embarrassed
to admit it, even to yourself. It's a special, open-ended kind of pain,
like having a disease that doesn't even have a name. You worry you
must be pathetically oversensitive to feel so wounded over such a
thing. You can't tell people, "My friend broke up with me," without sounding like a nine-year-old. The only phrase I can think of
that even recognizes this kind of hurt—"You look like you just lost
your best friend"—is only ever spoken by adults to children. You
can give yourself the same ineffectual lecture your parents used
to give you as a kid: anyone who'd treat you this way isn't a very
good friend and doesn't deserve your friendship anyway. But the
nine-year-old in you knows that the reason they've ditched you is
that you suck.

I've replayed conversations and incidents from my friendship
with Felix in my head, cringing at things I said or did that might've
been stupid or thoughtless or insulting. But all my private theories
are pretty obviously projections of my own insecurities, and they
still amount to a perverse kind of vanity; whatever happened with
him probably had less to do with me than I imagine. It's true that
he'd acquired a serious girlfriend for the first time in years around
the same time he stopped talking to me, but the one time I met her,
at a wedding, she didn't seem like the kind of woman who'd try
to pry her boyfriend away from all his old friends; she wondered
aloud why we hadn't met before and said we should all hang out
sometime soon, the three of us. I left messages inviting them both
over for civilized, grown-up activities—dinner, a movie, a canoe
trip—but they never called back. And it's not as if he became a
different person, found Jesus, or entered a twelve-step program;
whenever someone unearths new evidence of his existence from

the Internet, it only confirms his unchanged Felixness: a photo of him with two pillows pulled over his arms, looming vampirically over the camera, a video of him pushing two squealing girls on a luggage cart through the corridors of a hotel late at night. The only thing he ever told me that gave me any insight into his disappearance was that he got tired of people too easily—little traits began to get on his nerves and he'd just leave. It was something he considered a character defect, but one he felt helpless to change. He was talking about the short half-life of his romantic relationships at the time, but I had occasion to recall it later on.

Over the years friends of mine have suggested various other possibilities, none of which sounded plausible to me: maybe he was afraid he was an alcoholic and thought I was a bad influence on him; maybe he was secretly in love with me. "Was he *crazy*?" my friend Abe asked me. "Not really," I said, after giving it some thought. "You don't think *Felix* was *crazy*?" said his wife, Margot, who had gone out with me years ago and remembered Felix well. "I'm sorry, man, but if you don't think Felix Harlan was crazy, you've lost perspective."

Admittedly, our friendship had always been sort of volatile. In fifth grade, Felix and Tom Weaver and I were all best friends. Three, as practitioners of statecraft and the polyamorous lifestyle know, is an inherently unstable number. We constituted a bitchy triumvirate of constantly shifting alliances, bitter enmities, and shaky three-way accords, employing the likes of Chris Schlemmer as double agents. Felix and I mocked Tom behind his back for a thousand little quirks and idiosyncracies, but, because I was nine, it took a couple of years before it occurred to me that they must be doing the same thing to me. To complicate things further, we were also the charter members of an organization called "The Comic Club," which was ostensibly dedicated to drawing cartoons but was mostly consumed in litigation over copyright infringements.

We were constantly defriending each other. "Defriending" (or "unfriending") has become a common term on social networking websites, where it involves discreetly clicking on a screen name to delete it from an electronic list, but let the record show that it was Felix Harlan, Tom Weaver, and I who originated it, circa 1977, and back then it was a deliberately cruel, face-to-face business. "Get away from us, Kreider," your best friends would say. "You're defriended." (The convention among the boys in fourth and fifth grades was to refer to each other only by last names, which sounded tough and manly and cool.) Oh and God help you if you got sick— you'd be absent for *one day* and return to school to find every boy in the class now united under the auspices of something called the Anti-Kreider Club, whose raison d'être was its dedicated hostility to all things You. One morning in sixth grade I showed up with an elaborate colored-pencil drawing of ancient Babylon—ziggurats, the hanging gardens, the tower of Babel—that I'd prepared for a group oral report on the ancient Chaldeans I was to give with Felix and Tom, only to be told they had defriended me again. Looking them in the eyes and smiling with the steely resolve of a samurai committing *seppuku*, I slowly tore the drawing in half. We all got zeros. It was a magnificent gesture and I still admire myself for it.

Each of the three of us had his own totemic animal—Felix's was the owl, Tom's the mouse, and mine was the polar bear—from which our fragile coalitions took their names: OP (Owl/Polar Bear) was Felix and me versus Tom, OM (Owl/Mouse) Felix and Tom against me. Notice that 1) the *O* always comes first and 2) there never was any PM or MP, and not just because it would've lacked a vowel. Felix was the fixed center of this triad, the one Tom and I each wanted to like us best, like a capricious child emperor for whose favor we courtiers were kept competing, cannily pitting us one against the other in Byzantine intrigues. Fifth grade is the last time I remember being unself-conscious enough to come out and ask a question like, "Who do you like better, me or Weaver?" But it wasn't the last time I wanted to know.

Why we put up with this treatment is a question only a grown-up would ask; anyone who remembers the heartless economy of grade school knows how fiercely we covet the affection of those who disdain us. Even though I often came home from school feeling like crying and drew cruel caricatures of him when he'd defriended me, Felix was my best friend. We've all gone through phases with roommates or road trip partners in which we speak in the same idioms, finish each other's sentences, and all but read each other's minds; Felix and I were like that for decades. We were often mistaken for brothers as kids, not because we looked alike so much as because we *were* alike. We didn't just have similar senses of humor; we had the same one, because they had formed together, like twins in utero. I could imitate his voice so well—it was less an imitation than like channeling—that he once asked me to impersonate him in a phone call to his sociology professor to explain why he/I would be unable to deliver an oral report on Monday morning. It was dodgy going at moments, but I pulled it off.

He was also the most hilarious person I've ever known—and I hung around with professional humorists for a decade. Unlike most comedians, he wasn't just quick at thinking up funny things to say or do; he was himself somehow inherently funny. He was always having to explain to authority figures—first teachers and later the police—that he wasn't being a smart-mouth or talking back; that was just how his voice sounded. He somehow looked insolent just sitting there, innocently doing nothing. Cops instantly recognized him as the enemy and tried to find some probable cause, which was usually readily available. In photographs of Felix taken decades apart—the high school yearbook photo of the Dungeons and Dragons Club where he's sitting at a table in the library with the touch of a smirk on his lips, a snapshot taken in a

Baltimore row house in the late nineties in which he's long-haired as Manson, retinas hellishly lit by the flash, displaying thirty-seven teeth in a demented Cheshire grin—you can see the same minor demon glittering out of his eyes. It's a barely suppressed hilarity, latent chaos, a readiness to loose anarchy upon the world as soon as the teacher's back is turned. The kid was trouble. I can still see him toppling out of his chair in the middle of reading class screaming, "Foot cramp!"; folding himself up into a bookshelf in the library and then being unable to extricate himself; leaping drunkenly onto the new ski machine at the Weavers' house one Christmas Day in college crying, "I'm Jean-Claude Killy!" and busting it. The day he dropped out of Boy Scouts, Mr. Weaver, who was his Scoutmaster, told him: "Felix, you're always gonna be on the outside, looking in." This prophecy came only halfway true.

Well into our thirties we continued to behave the way we had on sleepovers, except now with no adult supervision and legal access to alcohol. We'd be peaceably drinking in a bar when suddenly the dreaded Grappling would break out—a sloppy, spastic tussle that got us ejected from establishments not known for rigorous standards of conduct. We took forty-ouncers in paper bags to women's softball games, where we'd sit on the bleachers ogling the players. We once went stoned to midnight Mass on Christmas Eve, where Felix filled up a flask with holy water from a holy water fountain for his own obscure purposes, nearly knocked over a six-foot-tall candelabrum, and we went back for seconds on the host. One hungover morning at my house when Felix had stayed over, I was surprised, when I woke up, not to find him on the couch. I figured he must've gotten up early and driven home. I was making breakfast when I heard a small noise in my hall closet, as of something shifting or settling in there. I opened the door and Felix spilled out onto the floor in a loose tangle of limbs and hair. It wasn't until some time later, while we were eating breakfast, that he remembered what he'd been doing in there. "Oh, yyyyeah," he said. "You'd gone into the bathroom, and I was gonna leap out and *scare* you when you came out!"

There were some unhilarious times in those years, too. If you spend enough time careening drunkenly around county dive bars, bad things happen. Once, as we were passively watching a developing bar fight, Felix muttered to me, "I hope we don't get sucked into this like we always do." On one occasion I kind of got him punched in the face. And there was a grim week indeed when Felix, having totaled his second car in just a few months and unable to face his parents, holed up on my couch watching reruns of TV shows so terrible—a spinoff from *Three's Company* called *The Ropers* was a low point—that I began to fear for his sanity. One morning I had to go pick him up at a local correctional facility, where I found him limping, half his face abraded by gravel. We were both puzzled as to what he had been doing there. The last thing either of us remembered from the night before was seeing a Magic Markered

sign in the Rendez-vous Inn advertising two-for-one shots of Jack Daniel's. I took him out to breakfast at a diner, where he coolly ordered "the Short Stack" in a way that made it sound ob-scene.

I'd always thought of him as the kind of person who would survive a pogrom. He had zero respect for authority of any kind—on some level he simply didn't recognize its legitimacy, whereas I, to my shame, am too well brought up not to. If I were ever arrested I'd be scared and embarrassed, accepting in my gut that I must've done something wrong, and I'd try to be polite and compliant, hoping they'd treat me decently and let me go sooner rather than later, even as they loaded me into a boxcar. Felix, on the other hand, at the first sight of his old nemesis The Man, always immediately tossed his wallet into the bushes, noting its location for later, gave them an insouciant nom de guerre—"Malachi Stack" was his standby*—and watched for his first chance to escape. He was double-jointed and got to be adept at skinning the cat while handcuffed, slipping his arms under his feet to bringing them around front. He really did successfully flee the custody of the police, twice—once by slithering loose and vanishing into the roiling mobs of Mardi Gras, and once just by noticing, as he was sitting on a bench in a police station while everyone else was poring over a law book arguing over what to charge him with, that nobody seemed to be paying any attention to him, or the door. He just slipped out and hailed a cab. *mmwOWm*. It was this same self-possession that so shocked me when he vanished—his assumption of his perfect right to up and walk away.

Losing him meant losing an Alexandrian library of memories, old stories, and in-jokes: Felix smugly saying, "Mix up the animals, Tim," after winning another hand of five-card stud played for stuffed toys on a sleepover; Mrs. Gore's vast planetary rump eclipsing my writhing and terrified face, apparently engulfing my head as she accidentally backed into it in class; Felix wrapping his hand in toilet paper to retrieve a rubber-tipped dart he'd fired at me from the toilet bowl where it had landed, only to have his protective sheath transformed into a long slimy tentacle that he frantically tried to whiplash off his hand, flinging toilet water around the

---

*I learned only while this book was being copyedited that this was an allusion to Thornton Wilder's *The Matchmaker.* That fuckin' guy.

room; Tom Weaver sliding spectacularly into an open sewage line during a kickball game. We used to revive these stories periodically, retelling them to ourselves, honing and codifying them and fixing certain canonical details *(how Tom slid across the pool of sewage on one foot, sending a gleaming fan of blackwater into the air before him until his heel hit some impediment, a root or pipe, that abruptly sent him sprawling headlong through the sheet of spray, leaving a Weaver-shaped hole in it, and he plunged facedown into the muck)*, until I no longer knew whether I really remembered these things or only the stories. Without him, I'm like the last surviving speaker of a dead language.

I'd often drawn Felix as a character in my cartoons while we were friends—the wily-eyed stoner always advocating some insanity in judicious and reasonable tones. ("Maybe just one more and then that will be it.") It was hard to tell whether he was flattered or chagrined when strangers immediately recognized him from my caricatures. After he disappeared, I cast him in increasingly demeaning situations—as a corpse having his bare haunch eaten in a postapocalyptic bunker, his unhappy head impaled on a bamboo pole. Maybe I was trying to prod him out of his silence. But if he saw any of these provocations, he never reacted. He lost his speaking lines in my cartoons as his voice grew fainter in memory, but he persisted as a figure in the background for years after I'd last seen him, going through the same rote motions, as ghosts are said to do. It's still hard for me to believe that he isn't, some random morning, going to topple out of a door I've forgotten to check.

It's been suggested to me that I could just track Felix down and ask him what happened. He still lives in Baltimore; I even have an idea which neighborhood. I still have the disembodied head of what was officially called a "frustration pencil"—a regular no. 2 topped with a tuft of brightly colored craft-store hair, a black deedlee-ball nose, and plastic googly eyes—but which we all called "wubbles" when they were briefly a craze in our sixth grade class. I have given serious thought to tracking down Felix's current address and leaving the wubble head on his doorstep, like a grisly calling card. I know that when he got home and found it lying there he would immediately recognize this artifact, and that as he picked it up and looked it over, his eyes narrowing, the word *wubble* would enter his mind for the first time in thirty years and he would understand exactly who had left it there, and nod coolly, its message received.

The only flaw in this plan is that I would then be insane. Even hanging out in the dive bars in Felix's neighborhood and asking around about a Felix Harlan (or Malachi Stack) would be weird. The obvious impossibility of this plan illuminates something about the nature of friendship and its limits; after sixth grade, you simply aren't allowed to ask questions like, "Okay, Harlan, how come don't you like me no more?"

Defriending isn't just unrecognized by some social oversight; it's protected by its own protocol, a code of silence. Demanding an explanation wouldn't just be undignified; it would violate the whole tacit contract on which friendship is founded. The same thing that makes friendship so valuable is what makes it so tenuous: it is purely voluntary. You enter into it freely, without the imperatives of biology or the agenda of desire. Officially, you owe each other nothing. Laura Kipnis's book *Against Love: A Polemic* includes a harrowing eight-page inventory of things people are not allowed to do because they're in romantic relationships, from going out without saying where you're going or when you'll be back to wearing that idiotic hat. But your best friend can move across the country without asking you.

When you're a child, your best friend in the world is the kid who lives next door. It doesn't occur to you then that this is a matter of arbitrary circumstance. When you grow up you like to imagine that your friendships have a more substantial basis—common interests, like-mindedness, some genuine affinity. It's always a sad revelation when a good friend acquires a girlfriend or a husband and disappears. You realize that, for them, your friendship was always only a matter of convenience, a fallback, and they simply don't need you anymore. There's nothing especially cynical about this; people are drawn to each other because they're giving each other something they both need, and they drift apart again when they've aren't getting it or don't need it anymore. Friendships have natural life spans, like love affairs or favorite songs. It's just easier to be mature and philosophical about it when you're the one doing the defriending.

Currently my closest male friend is Harold—the same one who occasionally spots Felix in Baltimore. Even though we no longer live in the same city, he and I talk on the phone for at least an hour several times a week. These phone conversations are essentially the same as the ones I'd have with Felix for hours every afternoon during middle school, when we were no longer in the same classes; we're keeping each other company through a lonely time. Our conversations of late tend to begin with an opening statement: "A man has nothing." (This locution of referring to oneself as "a man" is one I picked up from Felix years ago, persisting like a whorl or cowlick passed from one generation to the next.) We bitch and commiserate about the emptiness of our lives, the absence of any available or attractive women anywhere in our foreseeable futures, the despair-inducing desirability of various unavailable women, exes, girls glimpsed on the street, and British actresses of the sixties. I have had to beg him not to tell me when he is Ironing the Pants, a rite he must perform each Sunday night before the next workweek that lays bare the absence of any hope or meaning in human existence. Last night I was outlining for him the latest of my implausible romantic schemes and he said, "Aw, you're gonna find happiness, and I'll be left Ironing the Pants of Despair." I was touched by how openly he admitted that he didn't want me to be happy. It's impossible for me to believe now that there may come a day when Harold and I no longer want to call each other all that often, and we'll have a hard time remembering what we talked about for all those thousands of hours. But for now, at least, we still have Nothing, except company.

Part of any friendship is ephemeral and contingent on circumstance, but there is another part, in some of them at least, that outlives the incidentals of your neighborhood or classroom, a part that is unkillable. During a recent visit home, on a nostalgic impulse, I

detoured through the development where most of my elementary
school friends had once lived. I got pleasantly melancholy driving past corners that had been my school bus stops every day for
years: there's where we picked up Nicole Rovner, with her fetish-
istic attachment to the color purple; there was the house of Drew
Blitz, whose head looked like a Q-tip. But as I turned up Milk
Thistle Way and approached Felix's house, I was startled by my
own response to the sight of that familiar driveway: my stomach
suddenly rose up with giddy anticipation, as though I were being
dropped off for a sleepover or we were about to go out and smoke
pot and Cruise the Night in Mr. Harlan's Impala, a car no doubt
long gone. It was as instant and visceral as the smell of your first
girlfriend's perfume, or the sound of the recess bell. Some part of
me still hadn't heard the news that Felix and I weren't friends anymore. It was like seeing a dog who can't understand that his best
friend is never coming home again leap up, suddenly young again,
at the sound of an opening door.

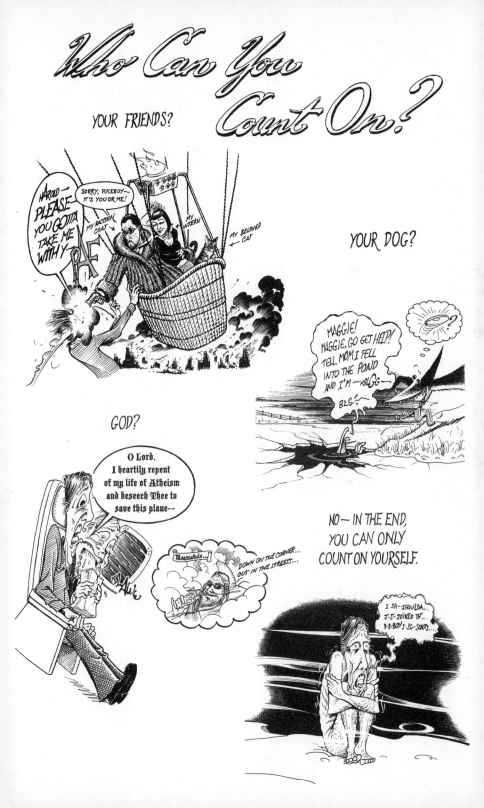

Escape from Pony Island

I'm forfeiting a friendship by writing this. It's a friendship that is effectively dead already, historical rather than active, but my concern is less with salvaging the relationship than it is to avoid hurting any further someone who feels himself to have been turned on and mocked by too many people already. But I know that no matter how empathetic or fair I try to be, Ken will read anything I write about him as a betrayal.

I know exactly what Ken thinks I ought to say about him, because when I told him I was thinking of writing about him he wrote a paragraph about himself and sent it to me. "I don't understand why you wouldn't simply say something like this," he said. There was something obscurely troubling about this; it seemed like making up a nickname for yourself or telling people that this is your new theme song and urging them to hear it in their heads from now on whenever you appear. He seemed increasingly unable to tolerate any perception of himself that diverged from his own.

I won't reproduce that paragraph here because Ken has since explicitly forbidden me to quote anything he's ever written. But it told the story of someone who became interested in a certain scientific debate, researched it extensively, and came to some alarming conclusions to which he tried to alert the people he cared for most. There was nothing inaccurate or dishonest in his description, but it used neutral euphemisms like "shared his reasoning" to describe what had seemed to me more like a campaign of strident and relentless proselytizing. For me, the last few years of my friendship with Ken had been like trying to remain friends with someone who'd undergone a Damascene religious conversion or married someone insane (analogies Ken would dispute at length). It meant having to accept something to which you're indifferent at best as an important new part of your friend's life, something to which they expect you to display an enthusiasm commensurate to their own. You couldn't say, "Hm, sounds interesting, I'll have to look into it," and move on to the next subject. There was no other subject. Ken spent years of his life and tens of thousands of words trying to persuade me and his other friends that our civilization was on the brink of collapse—a global catastrophe exponentially more enormous than the two world wars and all the pogroms and purges, epidemics and famines of the twentieth century combined. He staked so much on this certainty—switched jobs, sold his house, moved himself and his wife halfway across the country, alienated friends and family—that not to take it seriously was not to take *him* seriously. It was an impasse that ended with my giving up on a friendship I had once considered indispensable.

Here's how I would tell the story.

I used to refer to Ken as "the smartest person I know," and I don't think I'm the only person who ever called him that. As Michael Herr once wrote of Stanley Kubrick, "his elevator goes all the way to the roof." I'd met him more than twenty years ago, when I was his teaching assistant, and even after we were no longer instructor and TA I always felt as if he were the mentor and I the student. Just trying to keep up with him made me feel smarter. Spending time with him was not like spending time with most of my friends, a lazy relief from life, hanging out for hours drinking beers and thinking up funny things to say; it was an intellectual workout, hard and exhilarating, more like reading Conrad or listening to a Beethoven quartet. The conversation might've been recondite and wide-ranging, but it was never idle. You were not wasting time. And if that sense of seriousness and purpose occasionally felt like an imposition, it also turned out to be something for which I'd secretly been starved.

I never saw him meet anyone he didn't question in depth about their lives, their vocations and interests. They'd be self-conscious at first, but then become increasingly animated, trying to articulate answers to questions no one had ever cared enough to ask them before. It was hard to tell whether he was genuinely interested in people or if he was simply voracious for information, and regarded everyone he met as a new resource. Whatever the case, having someone pay attention to you with that kind of active intelligence made you feel as if your thoughts and experiences were valuable. Ken was someone to whom you wanted to bring your half-formed ideas and knottiest dilemmas. He was such an engaged listener, and so generous with his insight, that it could take quite a while before you noticed that you didn't know anything about his personal life at all.

Ten years after I'd been his TA, I reconnected with Ken when our friend Harold, who'd also taught with us, moved into the area. Ken told Harold and me that he wanted to organize an intellectual salon—a circle of brilliant, creative, and attractive people who would gather to discuss art and politics and ideas, collaborate and inspire each other. These people never showed up and the salon remained just the three of us, but for a few years our regular get-togethers were an important part of my life. Ken hosted long weekends at his house outside Philadelphia, for which occasions he always prepared good food—it was the first time I'd ever had coq au vin—and loaded up on music and films and piles of beautiful books from the library—it was through Ken that I first heard

Steve Reich's tape-loop piece "Come Out," watched the original version of Michael Haneke's *Funny Games,* and saw a collection of drawings by the French surrealist Roland Topor. We went on day trips to New Haven to see a Francis Bacon exhibit at the English Museum and an S&M, Starr Report–era version of *Measure for Measure* at the Yale Repertory, and to New York City to see Nicole Kidman in *The Blue Room.* And once a year we went on a long weekend retreat to Jane's Island near Chincoteague, which Harold and I referred to as Pony Island.

Ken would engage us in (or, sometimes, subject us to) long Socratic dialogues about politics, ethics, and art—I remember one, over venison steak, in which he challenged us to defend the taboo against incest, which left us sputtering in some uneasy state halfway between bemusement and horror, unable to articulate any arguments more compelling than the risk of inbreeding and anecdotal evidence of trauma. We finally fell back on the classic rhetorical fallacy, *For fuck's sake, Ken.* Moral philosopher Jonathan Haidt asks similar questions of his students in an exercise he calls "moral dumbfounding," to palpate the difference between reasoned judgment and visceral reaction. Understanding the distinction between the two is useful in clarifying ethical questions; simply discounting the latter, however, will get you stoned to death in the town square. In retrospect, Ken's straight-faced inquiry about such a touchy subject seems symptomatic of his overvaluation of pure rationality, a kind of emotional color blindness that would hinder his efforts, later on, to convince us of something just as hard to accept but far less hypothetical.

Ken was always a generous host and caterer, and he'd introduce us to great art and engage us in interesting conversation, but he always had an agenda, and eventually he would make us do work. After breakfast on Pony Island he'd ask us what we wanted to do, and we'd answer honestly that we'd be happy just to sit around the cabin drinking whiskey all day, and then the pretext of free will would collapse and Ken would haul us off our asses to go on a long hike, fueling us with a thermos of coffee, and subtly turn the conversation toward our next project.

It was talking to Ken for hundreds of hours about a film that he and Harold and I had all gone to see together that ultimately led to the critical essay that would become my first national publication. Ken prompted me to start thinking about the movie as sociological instead of psychological, political rather than personal—a film about wealth and power, not love or sex. In working on that essay we had detailed back-and-forths over fine distinctions of diction, connotation, and etymology that honed my prose. (I offered him a coauthor credit on the published piece, but he demurred.) It was also Ken who first pointed out to me the political implications of my early, absurdist cartoons. When he asked me whether I'd ever considered doing any overtly political work, I squirmed and resisted, complaining that political art had always seemed unavoidably humorless and didactic to me, and that it was depressingly perishable. I would later squander almost a decade of my productive life drawing cartoons about the Bush administration. He'd made me take my own work seriously, an unwelcome responsibility and a great gift.

It was in his expectations of how his ideas would be received by the world that Ken's perceptions diverged most radically from reality. He proposed that he and Harold and I go on a speaking tour to promote our film criticism, as if writers of critical essays ever went on press junkets. He urged me to prepare sound bite–length statements for the media attention we would soon receive for a parody of Pope's *Rape of the Lock,* about the Clinton impeachment hearings, that he'd written and gotten me to illustrate. Having spent several years self-publishing mini-comics, I knew exactly what would happen when we released this book: nothing at all. I'd always thought of publishing comics or zines as like radioing messages into interstellar space—more a gesture of faith than anything else—but Ken had apparently expected the effect of our booklet, which we'd personally distributed throughout the U.S. Capitol building, to be explosive. I would recall this odd naïveté years later during his campaign to convince us to take immediate action against the imminent fall of civilization.

He next proposed creating a comic book series called *The Host,* featuring superheroes based on the world's major religions, to be marketed to a conservative Christian readership. It was, I think, a pop cultural Trojan horse to sneak politically radical ideology into the evangelical market. My immediate response was 1) that fundamentalists would never accept a story with a pluralistic/poly-theistic premise, and 2) no way. Forget it. I had just come off *The Rape of the Dress* business, which had involved quite a lot of un-paid illustration work, and could tell that Ken was trying to sucker us into another intensive months-long project. And yet somehow, without ever quite agreeing to, we ended up working on it anyway. Ken often said of himself that he was essentially libertarian in his outlook, but Harold and I suspected that, like many libertarians, he was an authoritarian at heart. (People are most vociferously op-posed to those forces they have to resist most fiercely within them-selves.) Which is why our seminars so often trailed off into lectures, and why we found ourselves working for, rather than with, him on projects we'd initially refused to do.

Ken could never accept that Harold and I were authentic slov-ens. He must've felt, at times, like Lex Luthor trying to take over the world with henchmen like Otis. Once, during the short-lived *Host* project, he left the house to run some errands and charged us with outlining the plot of the first issue before he came back. Left to our own devices, Harold and I ate an entire bag of potato chips, helped ourselves to Ken's whiskey, and scanned his cable channels for nudity. We did manage, before he returned, to come up with the cartoon idea "Silly Negro—Trix Are for White People!" and I drew a preparatory sketch of The Veil (our Islamic superheroine) administering a blow job to a figure in a medieval plague mask. Ken seemed disappointed.

What Ken never understood was that the only thing Harold and I really excelled at *was* fucking around—coming up with idiotic ideas and filthy daydreams, projects like the pornographic version of *The Cat in the Hat,* the whitesploitation film *Kung-Fu Honky,* and our manifesto *Beyond Pants,* all of which served the sole artistic goal of cracking ourselves up. Ken was far more ambitious and disciplined than either of us, which is why we only ever accomplished anything under his impetus, but I think he also needed to harness our in-

spired stupidity to get any creative work done. Because the essence of creativity *is* fucking around; art is that which is done for the hell of it. And Ken was not a fundamentally playful person. His own artistic efforts were reverse-engineered to illustrate his political ideas; he once wrote a twelve-page script for a short film with an appended backstory/explanation/statement of intent that was at least twice as long as the screenplay itself. He and I both loved the novelty band the Upper Crust, but for different reasons: I just liked the fact that they dressed up in eighteenth-century foppery, but Ken believed they were subversively advocating revolution.

It was over such fissures in our beliefs about art and politics, imperceptible on the surface but penetrating to the core, that our little salon broke up. Ken indentured Harold and me into working with him on another critical essay that didn't interest me personally. I felt less like a collaborator on this one than an unpaid ghostwriter. In places his thesis seemed stretched a little thin. Things got testy.

Ken had written voluminous notes on the film, which I'd read over and marked up; next to one of his more abstruse digressions I'd written: *What the everlovin' fuck?* Ken was not amused. He called me intellectually lazy. I finally told him I felt he was projecting his own ideological agenda onto a film that had little to do with it. He burst out that a film is nothing more than a strip of celluloid with images printed on it, and there's nothing "in" it other than whatever we impute to it. I realized then that we had never been talking about the same things at all.

$$\mathcal{e}\mathcal{O}$$

This personal history is worth sharing because it all bears on our reaction when Ken came to us with an extraordinary claim: that the world we knew was about to end, and that we should join him in preparing for it.

Ken first mentioned peak oil to me when I was at a comics convention near his house in 2005. We were having lunch at an outdoor table when Ken asked me for my interpretation of the motives behind the Bush administration's invasion of Iraq. It is some testament to Ken's influence on my subsequent understanding of that war that I now find it hard to recall what my theories were at the time. Like a lot of Americans, I had no idea why our government had decided to invade Iraq; all I knew was that they had clearly been determined to do it since before 9/11 and that it obviously had little to do with the four or five filmy casus belli they'd run up the flagpole. My best speculation was to read it as a one-man psychodrama played out on the world stage: our commander in chief had always felt inferior to his baseball star/war hero/ex-president father, and wanted to both avenge and best him in a contest against Dad's old nemesis. Ken nodded in a pantomime of thoughtful listening, restated my opinion back to me in a fair paraphrase, and then began to outline his own "alternative explanation": oil.

This was typical of Ken's rhetorical strategy: a Socratic dialogue in which, as with the original Socrates, you are invited to offer your own opinion and quickly exposed as an ignoramus, whereupon he begins to explain the correct answer, putting forth whole systems of thought in long, well-organized paragraphs while you, relegated now to the role of chastened flunky, occasionally relieve his discourse with a dutiful "I do not know, Ken," or "Surely it must be so." Oppressive as I found this conversational style, I have to admit that Ken was right; in retrospect, it's obvious that the war in Iraq was over oil. Former head of the Federal Reserve Alan Greenspan admitted as much, with offhanded candor, in his memoir *The Age of Turbulence*.[1] It was a crude gambit in a twenty-first-century version of the Great Game with the entire globe as Risk board, a last savage scramble for the planet's rapidly evaporating petroleum supply. In the face of an imminent global energy crisis, the Chinese were investing heavily in the infrastructure for wind and solar power while the United States' best idea was to use its lumbering military brawn to seize the last major reservoir of the previous century's dirty, guttering fuel.

The term *peak oil* refers to the crest of the bell curve of petroleum production on this planet. After that point the supply of oil will only become scarcer and the price will (with occasional fluctuations) only rise, until the cost of extracting and refining it will exceed any potential profit. After which there won't be any more. When precisely this peak will occur is debatable; a lot of people believe we're already well past it. The biggest oil reserves on earth have been tapped; no significant new ones are being discovered. The most accessible and chilling analogy I've heard is that the situation is like being at a party where there's only one six-pack, we've already drunk four of the six beers, and it's after closing time.

So let's say we run out of oil. So we'll just switch over to wind and solar, right? We'll all ride around in monorails and zeppelins and tell our grandkids the Oil Age was too noisy and smelled bad anyway. Well, no, peak-oil theorists argue: no other single energy source, nor any combination of them, can come anywhere close to generating the levels of energy our current civilization demands. And the means of producing other forms of energy all require oil, from digging coal mines to building nuclear plants. Also, almost everything in our society is *made* with petroleum, from aspirin, toothpaste, and tape to eyeglasses, refrigerants, and anesthetics. And food. This is the truly scary part. Global food production—the agricultural equipment, the fertilizers, preservation, and, of course, distribution of food—is completely dependent on petroleum. It's no puzzle to biologists what happens to any population when its food supply is radically reduced. When it happens to animals it's called a *die-off*. But the implications of this equation in human terms are so unimaginably ghastly that most people would prefer to believe it's impossible rather than think about it at all. I keep remembering something the novelist Cormac McCarthy said in an interview: "If you were to take thoughtful people on, say, January first, 1900, and tell them what the twentieth century was going to look like, they'd say, 'Are you shitting me?'"[2]

Peak oil is not like the 9/11 Truther conspiracy theory or the Birther movement or any of the other currently fashionable delusional systems. The basic geological and economic facts of peak oil are uncontroversial: petroleum is a nonrenewable resource; eventually it is going to run out. We've burned through most of the planet's supply in less than a century, like crack addicts on a binge. What's less clear is what the long-term consequences will be, and how we'll adapt. Possible outcomes span the range of optimism from a somewhat hasty, perhaps not entirely bump-free transition to alternative fuels and energy sources, to the catastrophic end of our civilization and descent into well-armed barbarism. The darkest forecasts involve food riots, wars, and mass starvation, with deaths numbering in the billions.*

Ken is guarded about his own predictions, but it's pretty obvious he tends toward the pessimistic end of the spectrum, or else he wouldn't be lobbying so urgently for all his loved ones to prepare for the worst. Months before the economic crisis of 2008, he was predicting the collapse of the U.S. banking and financial system and runs on individual savings accounts, followed by gas and diesel shortages, followed by food shortages. He himself was selling off his own investments in stocks and bonds and buying gold. He advised me to keep several thousand dollars in cash or traveler's checks on hand, several weeks' worth of storable food and bottled water, as well as standard emergency equipment: candles, a flashlight, batteries, a hand-crank recharger. He was tentatively planning to relocate to New Zealand, where the "human-to-nonhuman biomass ratio" was lower, meaning that people will be slower to turn on each other once the supermarkets run out.

So far, it should be noted, not much has happened to contradict Ken's argument. Some of his specific predictions have been borne out by subsequent events, and the financial decisions he made based on his research have all been vindicated as savvy ones. He sold his house just before the housing bubble burst, at an 80 percent profit. He invested in gold when it was under $600 an ounce and silver when it was $11; as of this writing, gold is over twice that, at $1,240 an ounce, and silver is over $19. He was generous in sharing all this financial advice with his friends, me included, and we all ignored it. I never even bought a flashlight.

Ken always considered me one of the few people who'd paid attention to him and didn't simply dismiss him as a crank. But

---

*Please do not poison your children based on this information without at least conducting a little independent research of your own first. Bear in mind that I am simply parroting what Ken and other sources told me and do not actually know what I am talking about.

my main concern was making him *feel* that I was listening to him and taking him seriously. My focus was on the friendship itself, not the content of our conversations. I was like the dog in the Zen parable staring at the pointing finger instead of the moon. I read around in a perfunctory way on some of the websites Ken had recommended, attended a conference on peak oil for which he'd had paid my registration fee, and watched *Collapse,* a documentary about a leading peak-oil writer, at his urging. But I never did the hard, boring work of evaluating enough evidence for and against peak oil that I could make an informed decision for myself. I'd been evaluating all the information Ken sent me, but not on the basis of the facts; what I was evaluating was something else.

Ken was right: I'm intellectually lazy. I'm a fan of empiricism; it's just a drag to have to practice. If you're anything like me, you don't make up your mind about important issues by doing original research, poring over primary sources and coming to your own conclusions; you listen to people who claim to know what they're talking about—"experts"—and try to determine which of them is more credible. You do your best to gauge who's authentically well-informed and unbiased, who has an agenda and what it is—who's a corporate flack, a partisan hack, or a wacko. I believe that global warming is real and anthropogenic not because I've personally studied Antarctic ice core samples or run my own computer climate models, but because all the people who support the theory are climatologists with no evident investment in the issue, and all the people who dismiss it as alarmist claptrap are shills for the petrochemical industry or just seem to like debunking things, from the Holocaust to the moon landing. We put our trust—our votes, our money, sometimes our lives—in someone else's authority. In other words, most of us decide not *what* to believe but *whom* to believe. And I say *believe* because for most people, such decisions are matters of faith rather than reason.

But Ken is one of those rare people who actually change their minds—and their lives—based on abstract ideas, on books and intellectual arguments and evidence that challenges their beliefs. Such people are certainly a breath of bracing Enlightenment air compared to the much larger number of people who could care less about any objective pretext for their beliefs—who "just know" that Jesus is real or that Barack Obama is a closet Kenyan. You'd think that it would make them all the more credible to be free of any obvious agenda or emotional bias, motivated only by objective logic. But there's something off-putting about these hyperrational types; they're immune to any appeals to common sense or humor, the *for fuck's sake* defense. (Think of hard-core libertarians carefully explaining to you why the fire department should be privatized or heroin should be legal or everyone should be allowed to have automatic weapons.) As Kim Stanley Robinson writes, "An excess of reason is in itself a form of madness."[3]

A lot of peak-oil supporters seem to be of this genus, their decision making as carefully divorced from emotion as church is separated from state—which may account for their self-defeating assumption that other people are the same way. The typical rhetorical tone of the papers and articles on peak oil I've read is almost willfully unpersuasive, as if they're conscientiously refraining from any unfair effort to influence your opinion, instead simply placing the inert data before you and waiting for you to draw the correct conclusions. Ken forwarded me an article by Nate Hagens, editor of the peak oil-website The Oil Drum, called "Enter the Elephant," about the problem of overcoming the irrationality of human nature to effect social change. Hagens writes, "I am becoming convinced that confronting [people] with 'facts,' although necessary to better understand our predicament, will be almost completely ineffectual when it comes to altering our course . . . facts will become secondary and accessing raw emotions will be required for change."[4]

Reading this, I suppose I feel the same way Hagens would if I were to write an exposé breaking the news that we can't just make more oil. That this insight comes to Hagens this late in his campaign to educate a broader audience seems like a telling indictment of the peak-oil movement's inability to incite action. People are not sent screaming into the streets by warnings like "the global scale of financial leverage relative to achievable quality adjusted BTU flow rates going forward suggests significant changes to our per capita throughput, or even to capita itself,"[5] a sentence Hagens writes in the very next paragraph. It's hard to find a predicate in that sentence—it's the uncataclysmic "suggests"—let alone cause for alarm. (What this sentence appears to mean, roughly translated, is: "Smoke 'em if you got 'em.") At the peak-oil conference I went to I had the same feeling of walking in late on a conversation in which all the fundamental premises and terms had long since been agreed upon—of having missed out on the first day of class. By contrast, in summer 2009 Fox News was able to convince half the electorate that government health care would lead to some mandatory Carousel-like[6] festival of euthanasia.

At one point Ken wrote to tell me that he'd reserved a cabin on Pony Island, and invited Harold and several of our other friends and me out for a weekend of talking about peak oil—which, since Ken was the only person present who would have any interest in the subject, would mean a weekend spent *hearing* about peak oil. I imagined it being like one of those free weekends in Maui where you have to spend the whole time in a windowless conference room listening to someone try to sell you a time-share, tortured by the muffled sound of distant surf. I could picture my friends looking at each other, trying to keep straight faces, surreptitiously pantomiming suicide, passing notes saying *So hey man when's freakin' class over already?* I think I made an excuse not to go; as far as I know none of my other friends even responded.

Not everyone was as impressed by Ken's intellect as I was. My friend Lauren didn't necessarily disagree with his conclusions, but she rankled at his response: "Just write off the rest of society, drop out, and hole up in some compound?" I halfheartedly defended him: he hadn't abandoned everyone—he'd tried to convince his family and friends to join him or take similar measures. "Yeah well, if Ken's so brilliant," she said, "how about sticking around to help the rest of us figure a way out of this mess?" But Ken no longer had faith in institutions to recognize the problem, much less offer solutions. The time and money for technological fixes had long run out. And look at what had happened in Hurricane Katrina, he argued: the elites had abandoned the expendable population to fend for themselves. By the time we're shooting each other over the last can of corn on the shelf they'll be living like exiled emperors in fortified villas in Belize.

In 2007 Ken and his wife sold their house outside Philadelphia and bought property in a small town called Golden City, Missouri. Somehow I'd missed both Ken's marriage and his move to Missouri. By the time he announced both events we'd fallen out of frequent contact. Harold and I had gone to his engagement party and met his fiancée, but neither of us could make it to the wedding. And I'd moved to New York by the time he left Philly, and couldn't get away to see him one last time. Although I had legitimate excuses for both absences, the truth is that you don't miss such occasions if you're still close to someone. By the time you've realized that an era has a finite life cycle, an inevitable rise and decline, the peak has already passed.

After Ken moved to Missouri, we maintained contact exclusively through email, a medium that, as many have learned, is not conducive to discussing sensitive subjects or conveying nuances of tone. There was something relentless about his messages from Golden City, a steady, insistent pressure. He sent me long lectures about permaculture and biophysical economics. He waved off Rebecca Solnit's hopeful account, in *A Paradise Built in Hell,* of civil society spontaneously reconstituting itself after disasters, darkly invoking Hobbes instead. He repeatedly invited me to visit. Our correspondence began to remind me uncomfortably of conversations I used to have with a friend who was a cocaine addict: it always felt like he was trying to sell me something, to elicit some very specific response and would not let up until I'd given it to him. I wondered if this was what it felt like when someone was trying to seduce you. In my addict friend's case the pitch was relatively straightforward—I ought to sublet his apartment or buy this microwave out of the back of his car or just give him money with which to buy more cocaine—but I couldn't tell what it was that Ken wanted me to say or do. To admit unconditionally that he was right about everything? To sell off my stock in Smucker's and Rubbermaid and buy gold? To break my lease in New York and make immediate plans to move to Missouri and join him in the peak-oil compound?

Calling it a "compound" makes it sound more paranoid/survivalist than it was; he and his wife had bought a small farmhouse on four acres of land, where they were cultivating a garden and a "food-bearing forest" of fruit and nut trees. Ken was working for a small nonprofit dedicated to educating people about issues of peak oil, energy, and sustainable living. In the warm months, at least, their life sounded much pleasanter than the one they'd left behind on the East Coast. Ken wrote to me about the vegetables and fruits they were raising, the birds that visited their feeder, their new cat. They spent their weekends buying seeds, shopping for tools and tools used to repair tools. They were currently heating their house with propane and firewood but hoped to make the transition to firewood alone after installing a Franklin stove next season. In the meantime, Ken wrote, he was typing with gloves on. Reading this in my toasty New York City apartment, the radiator hissing pleasantly, I thought, *Yeah, no thanks.*

Writing him felt like a minefield of misunderstandings. It was increasingly difficult to avoid giving offense. I tried to anticipate and preempt his arguments. I'd pause and sit at my computer for twenty minutes, trying to think of a neutral, nonjudgmental synonym for what I really meant—*advocacy journalism* instead of *propaganda,* or *idiosyncratic* instead of *batshit*—that would not provoke a paragraph-long rebuttal parsing my word choice and deconstructing my meaning—only to have him seize on my revised words and write paragraph-long rebuttals of them instead. ("Can you explain to me how anything I've done could be accurately described as 'idiosyncratic'?") If I called his crusade "Cassandran" he would prove to know much more about the history of the myth of Cassandra than I did and could easily demonstrate why my analogy was false in five different ways. It was one reason I'd always admired and deferred to him—he knew so much more than me, about everything. But he never seemed to understand that exhausting someone in argument isn't the same as convincing them. In fact it frequently accomplishes the opposite. "Ken might be right, I'll give him that," admitted my friend Kevin. "But I'm never, ever going to agree with him."

Even when you were trying to agree with him, it seemed as if you could never agree *enough*—you were always going to be behind the curve, things were always worse than you understood. I'd forward him an interview with the political science-fiction writer Kim Stanley Robinson in which he referred to peak oil, and Ken would respond that it was nice to hear that Robinson was catching up but he was disappointed that he seemed unaware of the even more pressing issues of peak water and peak phosphorus. Like, now I'm supposed to worry about peak *phosphorus?* It was becoming easier to ignore him than to try to keep up. His worldview was gradually contracting into a one-man club—or two people, including his wife—that excluded everyone else on earth.

Ken and his wife endured more social ostracism over the issue of peak oil than my friend Jim Boylan did when he announced that he was going to become a woman. (Maybe most people—most liberals, at least—are less inhibited about judging people for what they believe than for what they are.) According to Ken, he had been mocked by his closest friends and family. His in-laws had openly urged his wife to leave him, telling her that her husband was insane, that he'd hijacked her life on some delusional crusade. ("People don't move *to* Missouri," her mother explained.) Ken had reason to be oversensitive. But I also think he engendered some of this defensiveness and hostility because his life choices seemed to a lot of people—whether he intended them as such or not—like tacit repudiations of their own. He made the rest of us look complacent, lazy, indulgent, and apathetic, in the same way that vegans' conscientious diets can't help but indict carnivores' as callous. The impulse is to write such people off as self-righteous and shrill (which, conveniently, they often are) so that you can stop thinking about slaughterhouses and keep eating scrapple.

When somebody tells us something that would be disturbing or inconvenient for us to believe, we reflexively scrutinize that person for some excuse to discredit him. Their disdain for emotion and dogged, blindered focus on Evidence and the Facts makes it tempting to speculate that people like Ken, rather than simply being more objective than the rest of us—which might threaten to make us feel stupid—just have more deeply buried agendas and are driven by unconscious forces about which they're in even better-defended denial. It's not usually hard to find such ulterior motives in anyone, especially not in the sorts of people who are most likely to bring us such news. As soon as Ken started insistently telling us things we didn't want to know, all of his familiar eccentricities and foibles started to seem suspect, symptomatic of some pathology. Even those qualities we'd always admired in him—his unrelenting intellectual curiosity, his bottomless erudition, his adamant conviction—became grating.

His interest in peak oil was also consistent with a history of abrupt changes of direction in which he'd reorganize his whole life around some new intellectual enthusiasm. Once every five years or so he'd change his academic focus, his career, and his circle of friends. He'd amassed a BA, two MAs, and an MFA, and begun two PhDs and abandoned them both ABD (all but dissertation). One day when we were driving from my cabin down to Ken's house, Ken in one car and Harold and me following, Ken unexpectedly pulled over onto the shoulder, got out of his car, and ran back to ours. Harold and I thought he must be having car trouble, or had forgotten something back at my house. We rolled down the window. "I almost forgot to mention," he said, beaming. "I'm retired!" He ran back to his car and drove on. It was an uncharacteristic bit of theatricality. He explained further when we got to his house: inspired by his creative work with Harold and me, he'd resigned his teaching position and decided to become a full-time filmmaker. And he did indeed form a filmmaking collective, which made a few short films that were entered in competitions and festivals, until he discovered the implications of peak oil. So it's easy to hope that the peak-oil thing has almost run its course and by this time next year he'll be writing an opera about Eugene Debs or monitoring those mysterious radio stations that just recite numbers late at night.

But what most gave me pause, privately, was my sense that Ken was a deeply angry man. Which is not to say he was some stereotypical lefty ranting about The Man with the tendons in his neck sticking out; in fact his demeanor was exceedingly gentle and courteous. His voice was soft but insistent, reminding you of the way that some people lower rather than raise their voices when they're furious. I only ever heard him raise his voice when he concluded a long, carefully constructed argument, like an exuberant flourish at the end of a handwritten declaration, as if to say, "Refute *that*!" His anger, when he expressed it, was couched in deceptively bland expressions like "It puzzles me . . ." or "Can I ask you to be clear . . . ?" I'd lash back at his endless lectures from Golden City with what was, for me, real rudeness, telling him that he had done the worst disservice to peak oil that any teacher could do to his subject, turning it into an object not just of boredom but of active antipathy for me. He'd respond: "Fascinating insights, Tim."

I also couldn't help but notice that peak oil was something of a godsend to the frustrated revolutionary. Peak oil would be so *just*—a long-overdue, well-deserved comeuppance for global capitalism, an economic system predicated on infinite expansion finally crumpling against the limits of a finite planet, destroyed by its own delusions. And it's easy to imagine that a collapse would neatly cleave the Gordian knot of our society, clearing the ground for some vaguely imagined, more perfect future. Utopian fiction from H. G. Wells's *The Shape of Things to Come* to James Howard Kunstler's peak-oil novel *World Made By Hand* (which depicts the postindustrial era as "an enlightened nineteenth century") often relies on some handy cataclysm to set the stage for the writer's own Potemkin paradise. It's an abdication of authorial imagination in the face of the messy present, the insoluble problem of the world.

And peak oil conveniently threatens the very power structures for which Ken has always had such passionate loathing. He mistrusted any form of institutional authority, from the government to corporate capitalism to the family. He boycotted a biopic about Queen Elizabeth because it glorified monarchy, and brushed aside my halfhearted arguments about historical context: "It was a brutal, oppressive system, and plenty of people living at the time knew it and said so." I remember an argument in which Harold and I tried to convince him that children needed parental supervision and rule, at least up to a certain age, if only to keep them from crossing the street against the lights. Ken obstinately insisted this was a myth used to justify patriarchal oppression. I couldn't help but wonder whether, beneath his pro forma claims to be as appalled as anyone at the prospect of our civilization's self-destruction, there was not a secret parricidal satisfaction.

But it's easy to dismiss anyone's argument with armchair psychoanalysis. Rebecca Solnit challenges our culture's presumption "that the proper sphere of human activity is personal, that there is no legitimate reason to engage with public life, that the very act of engaging is juvenile, blindly emotional, a transference of the real sources of passion."[7] And I mistrust the relief that this line of thinking affords me. Clearly I'm eager to believe that Ken just has an ideological axe to grind, or some neurotic personal investment in peak oil, because if he is deluded, and all I have to worry about is a friend going crazy, it means I can go back to scheming various long-shot seductions and wondering whether the *Captain America* movie will be any good instead of putting solar panels on my cabin and learning how to garden, at which I have always sucked.

It's comforting, for this reason, that so many peak-oil theory supporters seem to be outsiders—the people with the least invested in the status quo and the ones who might most like to see it in a shambles. But if some imminent threat to the sociopolitical order *were* to come along, it would only make sense that the people who'd been vigilantly watching for one for so long would be the first to see it. We regard those guys who patrol beaches with metal detectors as amusing eccentrics, but if there are any lost Bulova watches or gold doubloons buried out there, it's going to be one of them who finds them. Ken's contempt for authority, his disdain for emotion, and his humorlessness on this issue may give him greater clarity than the rest of us. We think of color blindness as a defect, but it enables those afflicted with it to see through camouflage.

So even though Ken may have some, yes, idiosyncratic opinions on certain subjects and plenty of personal motive to misread reality, he remains one of the smartest people I've ever known. And if he's correct, his behavior is completely appropriate. Imagine that you were a time traveler at a nightclub in Weimar Germany; could you really bring yourself to make conversation, enjoy yourself, and avoid tedious and potentially touchy political issues? Wouldn't you, at some point late in the evening, corner someone you really

liked and advise them, in all seriousness, to forget about their involvement in the local Communist Party or Dadaist cabaret and
save up, borrow, or steal enough money for a one-way ticket to
Stockholm or New York? (Ken would insist he has no extraordinary prescience; he's just examined the same data that's available to
anyone and come to the unavoidable conclusion.) The way he acts
is exactly how you'd hope to behave in such a situation: struggling
to control your increasing impatience and maintain a reasonable
demeanor, but refusing, no matter how bored or annoyed everyone
around you gets, to stop trying to convince your friends to listen
to you. It might well make you preachy and mad if you'd learned
that everyone you knew was in imminent mortal peril and you
tried to warn them and they all kept twirling their fingers at their
temples when they thought your back was turned. Ken's been a lot
more tenacious and selfless than I would be in his place. The first
time anyone made fun of me I'd say *fine* and imagine turning them
away from my cabin with a shotgun when they came begging for
a can of cat food.

It's funny—we all grow up on a diet of stories about the lone
voice of reason trying to warn everyone about some imminent ca-
lamity, from Noah to Jor-El, and instinctively side with this hero
and despise the ignorant ovine masses who jeer him or try to silence him. And yet whenever such a person appears in real life, our
reflex is to join in with the mobs of scoffers and call them alarm-
ists, hysterics, conspiracy freaks, and doomsayers. Nietzsche wrote,
"One often contradicts an opinion when it is really only the tone
in which it has been presented that is unsympathetic."[8] Or, as The
Dude put it: "You're not wrong, Walter—you're just an asshole."[9]
Less quotable, and often overlooked, is Walter's response: "Okay,
then." The Walters of the world don't *mind* being assholes; what
matters to them is being right. Visionaries, prophets, and revolu-
tionaries aren't concerned with good manners, being nice, fitting in;
what they're concerned with, passionately, singly, often monoma-

niacally, is the truth. "It's popular to think the world gets changed by delightful people," as Rebecca Solnit says, "but agents of change are often obsessive, intransigent, unreasonable, and demanding." [10]

Which makes them bad dinner guests, and a drag at parties. They are the dreaded Political Bore—didactic, hectoring, and humorless, that guy who, once set off on his obsessive pet topic, can't be diverted from it or made to shut up. You try to look thoughtful and interested and nod occasionally so that he thinks he's winning you over when what you're really doing is waiting for him to pause long enough between clauses for you to make an excuse about getting another beer so you can get the hell away from him. One email Ken sent me in response to my request to come visit his farm in Golden City to write about his life there—an email whose upshot was "no"—ran to 3,800 words. When printed out, it came to nine single-spaced pages. There was nothing unreasonable in this email; what's unreasonable is sending someone a nine-page-long email. But this was the sort of thing you couldn't explain to Ken. My position on peak oil was never that Ken was wrong; my position was, *Please shut up.*

But boredom is seldom as uncomplicated as a simple lack of interest; it's more often a numbing cover for something deeper. It may be that we all got so sleepy and irritable whenever Ken started talking about peak oil because We Couldn't Handle the Shit Ken Was Laying Down. Maybe I prefer not to think about it for the same reason it's easy to convince myself that that noise in my car's driveshaft, or the twinge in my molar, is probably nothing and will soon go away. If Ken is wrong, I get to feel superior and sorry for him; if he's right, it means I have to be afraid.

Peak oil is an awkward topic. In trying to explain it to acquaintances, I always feel like I'm bringing up pedophilia or clitoridectomies. It's a buzzkill to say things like "mass starvation" or "die-off in the billions" when people are trying to enjoy their beers. But Ken isn't especially interested in sparing anyone's sensibilities. Beneath

his studied politeness there is an uncompromising, hard-assed mo-
rality. He once introduced me to a lovely Chinese cartoonist, a professional political satirist who nonetheless parroted the party line
when Ken questioned her about Tibet: the Tibetans were a very
primitive people before the Chinese arrived, she explained, living
in unsanitary conditions, illiterate, practicing slavery. The Chinese
had made many improvements in their standard of living, building infrastructure and schools. The Tibetans should be grateful to
them. I watched as Ken gently interrogated her: "Do you think
the Tibetans would say the same things that you're telling me?"
he asked. "Do the Tibetans *want* the Chinese there?" She was not
fluent in English and I had to watch as she mentally translated all
this and got first confused, then increasingly guarded and defensive. I suppose she was as unused to hearing her state propaganda
challenged as most pretty girls are to being told that they don't
know what they're talking about. Eventually she retreated into a
surly, petulant silence and Ken finally relented, laughing and telling her, in the overly enunciated voice Americans use with foreigners, "Melei, you've lasted *much longer* without getting angry at me
than most people ever do." She wasn't laughing.

As the audience to this exchange, I could only cringe in admiration. I am much too polite to confront a guest in this country about
her government's policies, and too gallant and lecherous to risk of-
fending a pretty girl. But Ken was right: the Chinese don't belong
in Tibet. It's not their fucking country. This conversation serves as
a useful mirror for observing my own reactions to Ken. Like most
mirrors, it is not flattering. I can't help but wonder whether, in my
exasperation with Ken's impolitic style, I'm not reacting with the
same angry defensiveness as that cartoonist at having my comfy
ideological assumptions challenged—because he's making me look
at aspects of my life I'd prefer to leave unexamined. In other words,
What's *my* Tibet?

My final break with Ken came the morning after Election Day,

2008. I had volunteered for the Obama campaign, going door-to-door in public housing projects to register voters and make sure people went to the polls. I lived in Clinton Hill, Brooklyn, an historically black neighborhood that became one of the epicenters of celebration in America when Obama won that night. People were dancing in the streets. Again and again you heard people saying into their cell phones, "There's a brother in the White House." Black guys in pimped-out rides were honking in solidarity at me just because I was wearing an Obama button. DeKalb Avenue was filled with celebrants; cars were surrounded and trapped as if in a flood. A large black policeman waded into the street, gamely trying to get everyone to disperse so traffic could get through, when suddenly someone lunged at him and hugged him. The crowd converged on him—suddenly *everyone* was hugging him, a massive pileup of love. He started laughing. Neighborhood matrons who'd been born long before the civil rights movement were standing on their front steps taking it all in, slowly shaking their heads.

The next morning, as I was waking up in a new world, trying to come to grips with disorienting emotions like national pride and faith in my fellow men, I received an email from Ken informing me that anyone who was excited or hopeful about Obama's election was a "simpleton" because no one individual or policy initiative could alter the irrefutable scientific facts of . . . you-know-what.

In retrospect, I think that Ken's focus had become so exclusive, his sources of information so insular, and his community so closed that he could no longer imagine the emotional context into which he was dispatching his message. But that morning it was hard to read it as anything other than a gratuitous *Fuck You* greeting card, like showing up at a funeral just to let the assembled mourners know the deceased was a son of a bitch and you for one are glad to be rid of him. I wrote Ken back and told him flatly that I'd had it; I never wanted to hear anything he had to say about peak oil again.

He politely agreed to abide by my ban and asked me to let him know if there were any other topics that were off-limits. The flattening effect of email made it impossible for me to tell whether this affectless reply was Aspergerian cluelessness or passive-aggressive bullshit, but by then I didn't care anymore. It turns out that our internal resources are not infinite, either, and can be depleted to the point of exhaustion.

None of this actually has any bearing on the facts of peak oil. Some matters of empirical fact are independent of our ideology or biases, one of them being how much petroleum is left on the planet. Ken may indeed have some personal stake in the phenomenon of peak oil, but peak oil has no reciprocal relationship to Ken. The facts are just out there being placidly factual, unconcerned with Ken's or my or anyone else's feelings about them. Some people blamed the Black Death on witches, some on physicians for meddling with the will of God. In fact it was caused by the bacillus *Yersinia pestis,* a bacterium transmitted by fleas, and it killed a third of Europe.

So what you probably want to know is: what's the verdict on peak oil? Can we just call Ken and his cohort a bunch of crackpots and go back to thinking about social media and the Tea Party and the sexy teen vampire craze (all subjects, as of this writing, widely considered interesting and significant by the U.S. media)? Or should we be pricing cheap land in the country, buying up canned goods and tools, and learning to, like, till the soil? Is it really possible that the coming century—maybe even the next decade—will see the collapse of the global economy, world wars, and the deaths of billions? Is this idiot glittering din that we call our culture just a last frantic saturnalia on the lip of an abyss?

A better question might be: why are you asking me? As I may have mentioned, I never got around to reading up on the subject.

There is a reason you're reading my essay on this topic and not one of Ken's articles: who wouldn't rather read—or write—an essay about rhetoric and belief systems and a friendship's end than an article informing you that you and your children are probably going to die of starvation or cold unless you abandon the life you're living right now and take radically inconvenient action? But there's also a reason you really ought to be listening to Ken instead of me: I don't know what I'm talking about, and Ken does. I'm trying to hold your interest and amuse you; Ken wants to save your life.

He was always trying to find some way to bring his political message more directly to a bigger audience—hence his giving up academia for filmmaking, and filmmaking for direct activism. He was indisputably a great teacher, but he tried to turn life into school. The problem is that most of us hated school. His fallacy was much the same as progressivism's: the assumption that if he could just explain the facts clearly, build a convincing enough argument, eventually everyone would come around to his conclusion. But people aren't interested in lectures; they want to hear stories. Which is why the right holds the demagogic advantage over the left in America; they tell a simpler, more satisfying story. And it's one reason I've told Ken's story here. I fear he'll see this essay as a betrayal, the former pupil taking a shot at his overbearing mentor (talk about parricidal motives), but what it's ended up being is an attempt, in my own emotional, intellectually lazy way, to carry on his agenda. I am still working for Ken.

Ken was painfully aware, as he watched his family and friends abandon him, of his own failings as a messenger. The same faculties that granted him his glimpse of the truth rendered him an unfit bearer of it. Prometheus didn't get a ticker-tape parade, either, you'll recall. The last time I heard from him was after he'd attended another peak-oil conference and sent out a mass email to impress upon his friends, once again, that peak oil was a real and imminent threat that would soon disrupt all our lives. I didn't reply. Later that same week, Procter & Gamble announced it would be raising food prices across the board to absorb increasing transportation costs.

I won't pretend to miss Ken's harangues about oil, but I do miss our old conversations, that sense of belonging to an elite intellectual underground—a salon—of taking myself seriously, thinking hard, and talking about things that mattered. I still wish I could email him to recommend films whose political subtexts he'd appreciate. When I recently drew a cartoon of the young newlywed royals being guillotined, I thought to myself, *Ken will like this.* I owe him more than I can say. The last and saddest lesson I learned from him is that most of us are motivated not by reason or even self-interest, but something more like middle school politics. In making up my own mind on the issue of peak oil, the most relevant question turned out to be not *Does the evidence support this theory?* or even *Is Ken trustworthy?* but *Would I rather live in the peak-oil compound with Ken or die in the food riots with Harold?* Harold and I have made our choice, if only by default; we've cast our fate with the doomed. He and I have agreed that, while our fellow Americans are looting Costco and we're barricaded in our favorite Baltimore bar, we're going to call Ken up and demand: *Why didn't you warn us?* It ought to be worth one last laugh. Maybe the vindication of apocalypse will have put him in a mellow and generous enough mood that even Ken will see the funny side. "I am resigned to being the butt of the joke," he wrote me once. "Until the punchline."

What's Your Plan When the Shit Hits the Fan?

KEN

HAROLD

ME

KEVIN

Babies Are Assholes

LET US IMAGINE THAT YOU HAVE A FRIEND
WHO HAS VERY POOR SOCIAL SKILLS.

HE IS NOT INFALLIBLY CONTINENT.

HE IS PRONE TO EMOTIONAL OUTBURSTS
AT SEEMINGLY TRIVIAL PROVOCATION.

LET US SAY THAT YOU WILL HAVE THIS
FRIEND FOR THE NEXT TWENTY YEARS.

The Referendum

An editor once called me because he wanted to commission an article about our cultural fixation on arrested adolescence. "Of course," he said dryly, "I thought of you." I gladly accepted the assignment, which sounded potentially interesting and paid well, but hours later I found myself brooding on our conversation, thinking: *Wait a minute, man—what do you mean, "Of course you thought of me"?* I should mention that this editor is an old college friend; we've driven across the country, brewed pineapple beer, and been pantsless together in several nonsexual contexts. He is now a respectable person, editor of a national magazine, a homeowner and family man; I am not. So I couldn't help but wonder: was there something condescending about this assignment? Does he consider me some sort of feckless man-child instead of seeing me as the accomplished figure I am—a cartoonist whose work is beloved by hundreds and has made me a thousandaire, a man who's been in a committed relationship for seventeen years with the same cat? The same guy who broke my collarbone in a plastic light-saber fight now considers me the expert on arrested adolescence?

My weird touchiness on this issue—taking offense at someone offering to *pay me money for my work*—is symptomatic of a more widespread syndrome I call "the Referendum." The Referendum is a phenomenon typical of (but not limited to) midlife, whereby people, increasingly aware of the finiteness of their time in the world, the limitations placed on them by their choices so far, and the narrowing options remaining to them, start judging their peers' different choices with reactions ranging from envy to contempt. The Referendum can subtly poison formerly close and uncomplicated relationships, creating tensions between the married and the single, the childless and parents, careerists and the stay-at-home. It's only exacerbated by the far greater range of options available to us now than even a few decades ago, when everyone had to follow the same drill: a job or housework, marriage, kids. So we're all anxiously sizing up how everyone else's decisions have worked out to reassure ourselves that our own are vindicated—that we are, in some sense, winning.

This tension may be less deep than class envy but it's also more acute, if only because it's so much more accessible. We're seldom exposed to the privileges of stupendous wealth except on TV, and mostly don't know what we're missing. But we can have lunch with people we grew up or went to school with, who drive the same kind of cars and live in the same neighborhoods we do, whose lives are as alien to ours as Keith Richards's or Kim Jong-Il's.

It's especially conspicuous among people who've been friends from youth, like that editor and me. Young adulthood is an anomalous time in people's lives; they're as unlike themselves as they're ever going to be, experimenting with substances and sex, ideology and religion, trying on different identities before their personalities set. Some people flirt briefly with being freethinking bohemians before moving back to the suburbs to become their parents. Friends who seemed pretty much indistinguishable from you in your twenties make different decisions about family or career, and after a decade or two these initial differences yield such radically divergent trajectories that when you get together again you regard each other's lives with bemused incomprehension. You're like two seeds that looked identical, one of which turned into a kiwi and the other into a banyan.

I may be exceptionally conscious of the Referendum because my life is so different from most of my cohort's; in my early forties, I've never been married and don't have kids. I recently had dinner with some old friends, a couple with two small children, and when I told them about my typical Saturday in New York City—doing the *Times* crossword, stopping off at a local flea market, biking across the Brooklyn Bridge—they looked at me if I were describing my battles with the fierce and elusive Squid-Men among the moons of Neptune. The obscene wealth of free time at my command must've seemed unimaginably exotic to them, since their next thousand Saturdays are already booked. What they also can't imagine is having too much time on your hands, being unable to fill the hours, having to distract yourself from the emptiness at the center of your life. (The constant external demands of frantic busyness provide a kind of existential reassurance.) But I'm sure that to them this problem would seem about as pitiable as morbid obesity to the victims of famine.

A lot of my married friends take a vicarious interest in my personal life, an interest that's usually just nosy prurient fun, but sometimes seems sort of starved, like audiences in the Great Depression watching musicals about the glitterati. It's true that my romantic life has produced some humorous anecdotes, but good stories seldom come from happy experiences. Some of my married friends may envy my freedom in an abstract, daydreamy way, misremembering single life as some sort of pornographic smorgasbord, but I doubt many of them would actually choose to trade places with me. Although they may miss the thrill of sexual novelty, absolutely nobody misses dating.

I regard their more conventional domestic lives with the same sort of ambivalence. Like everyone, I've seen some marriages in which I would discreetly hang myself within twelve hours, but

others have given me cause to envy their intimacy, loyalty, and ir-
replaceable decades of invested history. (Note to all my married
friends: your marriage is one of the latter.) One of those friends
cautioned me against idealizing wedded life, reminding me, "It's
not as if being married means you're any less alone." This sounded
to me a little like a rich person telling a poor one that money doesn't
buy happiness, but I knew what she meant. I also understand that
friends sometimes tell each other lies out of kindness—for example, that marriage isn't any less lonely, or that being single isn't
more fun.

Parenthood opens up an even deeper divide. Most of my married friends now have children, the rewards of which appear to be
exclusively intangible and, like the mysteries of some gnostic sect,
incommunicable to outsiders. It's as if these people have joined a
cult: they claim to be happier and more fulfilled than ever before,
even though they live in conditions of appalling filth and degrada-
tion, deprived of the most basic freedoms and dignity, and owe
unquestioning obedience to a pampered sociopathic master whose
every whim is law. (Note to friends with children: I am referring
only to other people's children, not yours.) They're frantic and hag-
gard and constantly exhausted, getting through the days on a sleep
deficit of three years, complaining about how busy and circum-
scribed their lives are, as though they hadn't freely chosen it all.

Not long ago, when I was staying with some friends who have a
young daughter, one of them tiredly reported that there were more
"pee clothes" to add to the laundry, and then thought to ask me if
I had anything I wanted to throw in the wash. I answered, not to
be a smartass but in simple truth: "Not with pee clothes." She gave
me a look best transcribed as: *Oooo, lookit* Mr. Fancy! *Too fastidi-
ous to have his precious raiment washed with a little girl's pee clothes.* I
suppose "No, thanks" would have been the polite response. I have
noticed that parents of young children seem to take some gratuitous enjoyment in discussing what they persist in calling, even in

the company of other adults, "pee" and "poop," like veterans swapping stories of battlefield grue to horrify civilians. But, as another friend who also has young children later explained to me, one side effect of parenthood is the dissolution of all personal boundaries, like squeamishness about our bodily functions. What my friend was really telling me with her laundry offer, which I was too preoccupied with my own Referendum to hear, was that I was family.

I have never even idly thought for a single passing second that it might make my life nicer to have a small rude incontinent person follow me around screaming and making me buy them stuff for the rest of my life. (I already have several *large* rude incontinent friends, one of whom is bugging me to buy him a first edition of Ray Bradbury's *Dark Carnival* and another who thinks I owe him a Cadillac.) But one reason my friends with children sometimes envy my life, and I never envy theirs, is that they know what they're missing, and I don't. There are moments when some part of me wonders whether I am missing not only the whole biological point—since reproducing is, evolutionarily speaking, the one simple job we're supposed to accomplish while we're alive—but something else I cannot begin to imagine, an entire dimension of human experience undetectable to my senses, like an inhabitant of Flatland scoffing at the theoretical notion of *sky*.

And I can only imagine the paralyzing terror that must seize my friends with families as they lie awake calculating mortgage payments and college funds and realize that they are locked into their present lives for further into the future than the mind's eye can see. Judging from the rote unanimity with which parents preface any gripe about children with the disclaimer "Although I would never wish I hadn't had them and I can't imagine life without them," I can't help but wonder whether they don't have to repress precisely this wish on a daily basis.

I have no real interest in people's rationales for getting married or having kids, or for not doing so. I suspect people reproduce for exactly one reason—biology—and decline to for another—pathology—and I'm thankful my own modest pathology exempts me from having to handle feces or see Disney films or pretend to care about soccer. Nothing anyone says in defense of such major, irrevocable life choices is likely to be their real reason for making them; the number and vociferousness of our rationales is only an indication of how irrational and primal those decisions are. What interests me is the need to offer such justifications, to validate ourselves at the expense of others.

Yes: the Referendum gets unattractively self-righteous and judgmental. Quite a lot of what passes itself off as a dialogue about our society consists of people trying to justify their own choices (pursuing a creative career instead of making money; breastfeeding over formula; not having children in an overpopulated world) as the only right or natural ones by denouncing others' as selfish and wrong. So it's easy to overlook that it all arises out of insecurity. Hidden beneath all this smug certainty is a desperate cluelessness, and the naked 3 A.M. terror of regret.

The problem is, we only get one chance at this, with no do-overs. Life is an unrepeatable experiment with no control. In his novel about marriage, *Light Years,* James Salter writes: "For whatever we do, even whatever we do not do prevents us from doing its opposite. Acts demolish their alternatives, that is the pardox."[1] A colleague of mine once hosted a visiting cartoonist from Scandinavia who was on a promotional tour. My colleague, who has a university job and a wife and children, was clearly a little wistful imagining that cartoonist's tour—sleeping on couches in Brussels, Paris, and New York, meeting fans and colleagues (some of them pretty girls, maybe), being taken out for beers every night. Meanwhile the cartoonist, who looks very much like one of the gangling anthropomorphic birds he draws, looked forlornly around at his host's pleasant row house and sighed, almost to himself: "I would like to have such a house."

One of the hardest things to look at is the life we didn't lead, the path not taken, potential left unfulfilled. In stories, those who look back—Lot's wife, Eurydice—are irrevocably lost. Looking to the side instead, to gauge how our companions are faring, is a way of glancing at a safer reflection of what we cannot directly bear, like Perseus seeing the Gorgon safely mirrored in his shield. It's the closest we can get to a glimpse of the parallel universe in which we didn't ruin that relationship years ago, or got that job we applied for, or made that plane at the last minute. So it's tempting to read other people's lives as cautionary fables or repudiations of our own, to covet or denigrate them instead of seeing them for what they are: other people's lives, island universes, unknowable.

Not long ago I received a text message that read: ZELDA'S FEELING BETTER BUT SHE DIDN'T GO TO BALLET, SO YOU DON'T HAVE TO PICK HER UP. For an instant it was like one of those nightmares where it's the final exam for a course you'd forgotten you ever enrolled in. Had I been *supposed* to pick up Zelda after ballet? My plan had been to spend the afternoon at Grand Central's Oyster Bar with my friend Rick. Who *was* Zelda? Then it made sense: Zelda was the daughter of my editor friend—the same one who'd asked me to write the essay on adolescence. His wife had sent me the message by mistake. It was like an accidental glimpse into one of those alternate realities—one in which my schedule was crammed with responsibilities, my life trammeled by love. I wrote her back to let her know she'd misdirected her text, and then forgot about it, the way you wake from a dream or snap out of a moment's reverie. Rick was sauntering across the floor of the main concourse, late as usual, a hand raised in greeting. One of the benefits of Rick's company, which lasts exactly as long as you're in his presence, is the feeling that whatever you are doing is preferable to anything anyone else on earth is doing at that moment. It was time for lunch.

Bad People

One Saturday morning when I was in my teens, my father called upstairs for me to get up because we had to get dressed for his younger brother's wedding. I called *Okay* then fell back asleep. He called up again, then knocked on my door several times. I said *I'm up I'm up I'm up* and slept on. Finally, Dad entered my room.

"Dad," I told him, "I really don't want to go to Uncle Lee's wedding." He sat down on the edge of my bed.

"Do you know how many times your Uncle Lee has been married?" he asked me. I hesitated, leery that this question might be a trick one and also, come to think of it, not sure of the correct answer. I knew Uncle Lee had been married once, to my aunt Liz. He was the first person I'd known to get divorced. But hadn't there been another wife in there somewhere? An overcheerful, deluded-seeming blonde—Aimie? Angie? Or had she just been a girlfriend?

"No?" I said.

"Well," my dad said, "I'm not sure he does, either," and got up.

I woke up a couple hours later and was surprised to find myself alone in the house. It took me a few minutes to absorb that my father had, uncharacteristically, let me off the hook. I remember this episode fondly not only because it was one of the few times I was excused from some boring family function but because it was also the first time I could remember my father taking me into his confidence to side, even jokingly, against his brother, or acknowledging that his loyalty to him had its limits.

My father and my uncle Lee were like two brothers in a fairy tale—much alike, one light, one dark. The overachiever and the fuckup; the favorite and the disgrace. My father, Walter, was what you might call extremely high-functioning, hypercompetent, a man who always seemed to have two or three appointments scheduled at once. If there were such a diagnosis as unipolar mania I'd almost wonder whether he'd had it. "Some who knew him found him slightly unsettling," a columnist friend of his wrote after he died, "for he was constantly on the go and threw off ideas the way a burning pine log throws sparks."[1] He was chief of staff health at John Hopkins Hospital and later joined the World Health Organization, speculated in real estate and led local efforts in land preservation, served on several church boards and committees, cofounded a religious retreat center, and took us on ambitious family vacations, renting out a Winnebago to drive out west and hiring a boat to cruise the Chesapeake Bay. His brother Lee was bipolar, and died in prison.

My father was handsome, charismatic, and funny, quick with silly jokes and puns, and a dapper, but not flashy, dresser. My friends called him "dashing." He was such a large personality that *Dad* was an adjective in our family: "It was a very Dad way to handle it." Lee was good-looking in a seedy, Robert Mitchum kind of way, with sideburns, a dimpled chin, and a sly slope to his eyes that suggested he was always scheming something, figuring the angles. (A friend of mine, looking at an old photo of him, said: "He looks like a supporting character in a seventies movie about muscle cars.") Often one aspect of bipolar disorder is a compelling charm.

Lee used his the way anglerfish use their lights. I still don't know how many times he was married. He never seemed to have girl-friends, only fiancées. He would convince new acquaintances that he was a good guy who'd gotten some bad breaks and been cast out by his family, and they'd give him a place to stay or a temporary job and help him try to set up a life. (One well-intentioned character witness described him as "exceptionally honest and trustworthy.") Soon they'd be trying to rid themselves of this man as if he were a black curse out of the Brothers Grimm.

My parents agreed that Lee probably would've been a million-aire if he hadn't been insane. As it was, his life only ever amounted to a pathetic attempt to imitate my father's success. My father, as I've mentioned, was a speculator in real estate—"some of his conservation-minded friends . . . were disturbed by the rate at which he bought and sold attractive properties," wrote his colum-nist friend.[2] He also liked to go to auctions—I still have an an-tique post office cabinet and a stuffed sea turtle he brought home. Lee was an impulse buyer, too; a list of his assets includes a mobile home, a truck, an RV, several cars, boats, antiques, and various pieces of property. My father's investments proved sound: he made a lot of money off the sale of land and left his family a seventy-acre farm and a cabin on the Chesapeake Bay. Lee's buildings, trucks, and boats all rotted while he was in prison and ended up being sold off to pay his legal bills. As my mother put it, "Your father had some of that same manic energy Uncle Lee did. They were both full of ideas. The difference was that your father's ideas generally connected to reality, but Lee's never did."

My sister and I knew that our uncle had been in trouble with the law, in the shadowy, peripheral way that kids are aware of serious goings-on overhead in the grown-up world—the same way adults will vaguely register something in the news about a city-sized as-teroid passing within a thousand miles of the earth. "Uncle Lee got mixed up with some bad people" is how it was put to me on the one occasion when I asked directly. I was already familiar enough with my father's charitable euphemisms (he'd once described a street-corner drunk in Baltimore who'd mistaken him for an admiral as "very confused") to decode this. Even then I understood that my uncle Lee was the bad person.

Lee had been a problem since he was a teenager. He'd been sent to a juvenile corrections facility in high school, and his parents had sent him from Illinois to live with my father right after my parents were married, in hopes that his stabler older brother's influence would keep him out of trouble. It didn't help. The earliest documents I have pertaining to my uncle record a series of miscellaneous infractions—bad checks passed for an office machine ($833) and a '69 Camaro ($200), shoplifting (to wit: "did conceal merchandise valued at $7.42 under his shirt"), even a warrant outstanding from the U.S. Fish & Wildlife Service for "failure to obtain [an] oversand vehicle permit," which would appear to mean he was driving a car on the beach. It's the record of a man who couldn't seem to get through twelve hours without committing a misdemeanor.

On the two occasions I can remember being left in Uncle Lee's unsupervised company, he was ticketed for speeding and suborned me into littering. "Yeah, this thing'll fool ya," he told the cop who'd pulled him over, waving at his pickup's speedometer. Not even I, at age eight, was buying it. On the other occasion, when I asked him what to do with my candy bar wrapper, he shocked me by saying, "Just toss it on the ground—somebody'll pick it up." This was in the mid-seventies, when visible pollution was our most pressing environmental concern, and I had been trained by the weeping Indian and Woodsy Owl campaigns to see litterbugs as low types. But because he was the grown-up and I was the kid, I doubtfully tossed my wrapper on the ground. He once brought my sister and me a working nickel slot machine from a defunct casino as a present. His visits were like a whiff of cigarette smoke in church.

The Somebody'll-Pick-It-Up philosophy was evidently a governing one in Lee's life. The fact that all these overdue bills, bounced checks, and delinquent bank accounts ended up in my father's hands suggests that the mess of Lee's life was routinely turned over to him to tidy up. These scraps of paper sketch out a semilegitimate existence perpetually on the verge of disintegration: an envelope with a logo for "Accurate Scale & Equipment, Inc.," with the street address crossed out and "General Delivery" written in over it; a note to one of his girlfriends (addressed to "Honey Bunny") that reads, "Lots To Do Today But It's Raining And Mosquitoes Bit Badly Last Night In Truck Guess I'll Have To Use The Spot Up Camper & Put Up Mosquito Netting If I Can Park Less Charges." There is also, curiously, a bankbook for a savings account, created in April 1979, recording a deposit of fifty dollars. It isn't clear why this item was in my father's possession, as it is not in the name of my uncle, Lawrence Kreider, at all, but rather that of another person altogether, a foreign gentleman perhaps, by the name of Lorenzo Von Kreidler.

I should probably mention my uncle's handwriting here. It reminds me of a phrase used by mental health professionals: "floridly psychotic." Without reading a word of these letters you can see just from looking at them that my uncle is a lunatic. I'm just noticing, as I look at his writing, that it's not unlike my father's distinctively elongated and flattened hand—more like an architect's than a doctor's—but as if my father had taken mescaline about an hour before sitting down to write. Every word is capitalized, the capitals embellished with elaborate flourishes and curlicues, emphases added with double and triple underlinings, all conveying an affect of demented grandiloquence. Some of the O's are filled in with little faces, like the grotesques that adorn rococo architecture.

In a letter dated Easter Sunday of 1979, after an arrest on more serious charges—carrying a handgun and a concealed switchblade, assault, larceny of two postage meters, and "unauthorized use of a 1958 Studebaker"—my uncle charges my father with the responsibility of getting him out of jail. "I Will Eventually Return The Favor Including All Costs," he promises. "Now's Your Chance To Prove You Are A Man & A Brother. Try It, Lee." It's hard for me to imagine being anything other than disgusted by this pathetic hectoring, but here's a draft of a letter from my father to parties unknown—presumably Lee's lawyer, or perhaps the plaintiff—clarifying which of his brother's expenses he was prepared to assume and which he was not. "The family, having gone through a very similar ordeal twice in the past, finds this expense even more frustrating and extraordinarily costly." He assures them that Lee would be returning to a psychiatric facility immediately upon his release from prison. "I am enclosing a statement which I trust will be helpful in conveying our assessment of Lee's need for continued long-term psychiatric care and supervision." In a note that appears, from its raindrop-spattered ink, to have been left under a windshield wiper, my father gives his brother explicit instructions and conditions for the loan of a pickup truck, taking a rather more peremptory tone than you'd normally expect from one adult to another: "IT'S IMPORTANT THAT YOU MAKE TRIP TO WOODBROOK [the mental hospital] TODAY + BE RESTED WHEN YOU CHECK IN TOMORROW A.M." A letter from Lee's lawyer a month and a half later expresses surprise at learning that Lee has discharged himself from this facility, which was to have evaluated his competency to stand trial. A bill from the hospital was forwarded to my father.

"If he doesn't get himself into the awfulest situations," my grandmother wrote my father a few months later. "Am wondering what is going to happen next."

"ACCUSED" was the headline in the *Delaware State News* on August 30, 1981. "[THREE] PERSONS AWAIT TRIALS FOR THEIR ALLEGED ROLES IN SMYRNA COUNTY SLAY-INGS."[3]

It's strange to read luridly detailed newspaper accounts of a story I only ever heard in the vaguest, most evasive terms. Prosecutors described the three suspects in this case as "an assortment of social misfits." Ed Quarles was a nineteen-year-old who'd been discharged from the navy and was wandering on his motorcycle when he'd met Lee in Florida, who'd invited him to stay with him at his house in Delaware. When they arrived at Lee's house (which Ed later described as "a dump"), they found all the pipes frozen and burst. They went to do a load of laundry at Lee's friend Ilene Locklin's house and ended up crashing there indefinitely. From the first time Ed met her, Ilene talked about how much she hated her husband, a golf pro at a local club. By her account he was an abusive husband who'd beaten her, pulled out hanks of her hair, and violated her sexually with objects. (Ed later wondered, from prison, whether these stories had been true.) Ed, Lee, and Ilene would sit around Ilene's kitchen table at night, drinking beers and idly talking over murder plots they'd seen in movies and TV shows. They seem never to have explicitly agreed to kill Ilene's husband; they just casually drifted into discussing how best to do it. My uncle Lee suggested Ed, who had military training, for the job of offing him. Lee later assured prosecutors he would have gone to the police had he taken this talk seriously. While testifying against his co-conspirators, he said, "I guess you might say I sort of went along with it in a noncommittal way, as a friend of Ilene."

The murder was a black-comic fiasco out of a Coen Brothers film. The three conspirators had made several failed attempts on Locklin's life, including a staged mugging that their intended victim foiled by using his wife as a shield. Their final plan, elegant and foolproof, was to drug his food, bludgeon him to death in his sleep, and then place his body in the bathtub to make it look as though he had slipped and struck his head. Ilene crushed six Valium into a macaroni salad she served her husband along with peas and fish sticks. She left him asleep in bed to go let Ed into the house, but declined to stay and watch the murder. Ed clubbed Locklin over the head with a bottle in a paper bag, which instantly shattered and also woke him up. Ed, now armed with a bag of broken glass and confronted with a drugged and angry man, switched to the backup plan, pulling a knife and stabbing Locklin twenty-eight times. Then, reverting to the original script, he filled the bathtub with water and dumped the body in.

The police, finding a corpse with twenty-eight stab wounds in a bathtub, suspected foul play. Ed Quarles was arrested back in his home state of Minnesota two weeks later and made a full confession, trying to spare what he still thought of as his friends from implication in the crime. It was only when he learned that Lee was testifying against him that he began to understand that he had been used. The local papers made Quarles out to be the patsy and my uncle Lee the real villain. One article referred to him as "the mustachioed Kreider" and described him as appearing in court wearing a brown corduroy suit with an open vest. The same article noted that Lee refused to swear on the Bible, "saying he did not believe in the Bible." (This was not godlessness but a show of piety—Mennonites, citing Matthew 5:33–37's injunction against oaths, do not swear on the Bible in court but simply affirm the truth of their statements.) At my uncle's bail hearing, the deputy attorney general called him "a shiftless individual with no local ties and a tendency to violate parole and probation provisions." In a letter my uncle protested, "I Believe Someone[. . .]Should Point Out How Diligently I Was Working Towards Becoming A Well Respected Citizen Of Delaware."

My father retained counsel for his brother in May 1980. On the back of one of the legal firm's envelopes are several lists, jotted in his quick, precise writing. My father was an inveterate list maker—there's still one of his to-do lists on the brown paper backing the medicine cabinet door in my mother's house. His lists evidence a mind crackling with ideas, brainstorming, attacking problems from every angle. His notes on the meeting with Lee's lawyers include questions ("Why no preliminary hearings? Why were rights waived?"), potentially damaging information about Lee's codefendants ("Army/Navy—Paratroop Boots, *Soldier of Fortune* Magazine"), and ideas ranging from the immediately practical ("FAMILY SUPPORT—constant, personal, organized—a single strategy in coordination with a lawyer") to the less so ("*60 Minutes* [last resort]"). Most touching is his hope to rewrite the official story that made his brother out to be a reprobate: "Can newspaper image of 'drifter' be replaced with 'responsible, clean-cut Mennonite of good family'?" I doubt my father had any illusions about his brother's innocence (though who knows?—we're all adept at deluding ourselves about the people we love). But, if only for the sake of influencing public opinion, he wanted to try to make the world see him not as a shabby little killer but as an essentially good person who had gone astray, fallen into corrupt company. Gotten mixed up with some bad people.

"I Really Don't Know Where To Begin," Lee wrote my father after his arrest.

> "If It Were Only Possible For Us To Sit Down And Have A Long Heart To Heart Talk. It Is My Wish & Prayer That Somehow You Will Forgive Me For All The Trouble I Have Involved You In The Past Few Years."

This contrition would sound more credible had my uncle accepted any culpability or expressed any guilt for the man's death. Instead he was, as always, a victim of circumstance and others' bad faith: "It's So Hard To Believe Anyone I Tried To Help Out Would Do Such a Thing As Involve Me In A Crime I Did Not Commit."

"Walt," he writes, "I Only See Reason For This If I Have Been Called To A Prison Ministry Or Something."

> "I Know That This Last Year Has Been One Of Searching For My Place To Best Serve. I'm Sure There Must Be A Way To Put To Good Use All I've Learned The Hard Way These Past Years. I Wrote To Chuck Colson* To Inquire Of What His Efforts Have Been As His Work Has Been On My Mind For Quite Sometime."

Whether this was phony sanctimony calculated to ingratiate himself with his religious older brother or some genuine, if passing, impulse toward repentance is not for me to judge. My mother tells

---

* Charles Colson, former special counsel to President Nixon, once described as "the meanest man in politics," later a convert to Christianity and founder of the nonprofit Prison Fellowship.

a story about Uncle Lee once taking my father to task for mowing the lawn on a Sunday. Perhaps he was the kind of Christian who's a stickler for the commandment about the Sabbath but takes the one about killing on more of a case-by-case basis. For the record, Lee did not enter the ministry.

In December 1980, Lee's lawyers came to a plea bargain agreement: Lee would enter a guilty plea to the charge of conspiracy in the second degree and turn state's evidence against his co-conspirators in exchange for immunity on the charges of murder in the first degree and possession of a deadly weapon during the commission of a felony. It was an impressively favorable deal for a man who'd been facing a death sentence. However, he couldn't enter his plea until after his codefendants' trials, which meant he still had to spend several more years in jail. The letters from Lee over those years include bitter complaints about the incompetence of his lawyer ("I Got A Bill For The Only Collect Call I Ever Made To His Office. Bonafide Jew!") and the injustice of the state legal system ("I Think It Is Due To Fear And Capital Gain In A Nutshell!"). He wrote a letter firing his attorney that was never forwarded to the firm. There are crude inducements to guilt ("I'll Not Bore You With The Conditions Here But I'd Venture To Say If It Were You There'd Be 'Hell To Pay.' Evidently Apathy To Gross Injustice Is Universal"), sly threats ("If Nothing Else Works I'm Quite Tempted To Arrange Something Of Bodily Harm To Happen To Myself"), and, throughout it all, requests ("Be Sure To Bring Pens Next Visit & Gum, O.K.? $$ Also Helps!"). In a letter from my grandmother to my father, dated in late May 1981, in which she encloses the taxes on Lee's house, she writes that there's no asparagus this year, and the blueberries aren't doing so well ("Pete trained them too much"). An addendum is squeezed into the bottom line of the page: "Thanks for looking after Lee."

All this documentation comes from an accordion file folder stuffed full of old articles and correspondence concerning my uncle that my mother gave me when I was in my thirties. This was the first time that anyone in our family had even tacitly let me in on the whole truth about Lee. While he was facing the possibility of death on the gallows, I was preoccupied with *The Empire Strikes Back* and *Blade Runner* and making animated films with our home movie camera. At the same time that my father was dealing with this deluge of bills, outstanding warrants, continuances, legal fees, and demented letters, plotting his brother's defense strategy, and buying him radios and magazine subscriptions, he also bought me a then-state-of-the-art Super 8 camera with a single-frame button and a subscription to *Cinefex,* the trade magazine of special effects technicians. My sister and I were effectively kept insulated from the whole sordid mess.

I think my mother finally divulged all this sad family history as an unsubtle warning because, three years after my father died of cancer, Uncle Lee had started writing to me. The return address on his letter was a suspiciously long post office box address in the middle of nowhere, Florida. In the first paragraph, after a cursory inquiry into how I was doing, Lee got right to his main reason for writing: "I'm In A Bit Of A Bind At Present." "A Bit Of A Bind" proved to be something of an understatement. "I'm In Jail (Politics) The Good Old Boys Didn't Want Me Running Against Them." Further explanation was added in the margin: "So They Are Trying To Ruin Me. I Was Running For Sarasota/Bradenton Airport Commissioner (A <u>Very Good Position</u>)."

He really had been running for the Sarasota Manatee Airport Authority, it turns out. ("Candidate's been in trouble before," reads a story in the local paper.[4]) But there was a little more substance to the matter than "(Politics)"; the formal charge was twelve counts

of attempted murder by arson. This episode had apparently begun
as a rental dispute, wherein the tenants of a building Uncle Lee
owned had collectively protested what they considered unacceptable conditions and long-neglected repairs by withholding their
rent. Lee had boldly escalated the conflict by setting the building
on fire. Twelve people were in the building at the time, hence the
twelve counts. As with the assassination of the golf pro, it was not
the work of a Dr. Moriarty; Lee, who had fled the scene, was living
in his pickup truck with a couple of pit bulls when he was appre-
hended at a gas station, suffering from second-degree burns and
reeking of kerosene. If convicted, he faced a sentence of twenty to
fifty years.

"I Must Admit I Was Quite A Bit Disappointed When I Found
Your Mother & Lynn [my father's sister] Both Refused To Send
Enough Monies To Retain An Attorney For Me," he wrote. "Ac-
tually I Have No Idea Who Else I Could Ask. There Is No Way I
Can Get To Bank Properties Or Anything Til I Get An Attorney."
He claimed to own several boats, automobiles, furniture, jewelry,
"<u>Many Heirlooms</u>," etc., in Florida that could be liquidated to pro-
vide for his defense.

> *It Would Be <u>Extremely Helpful</u> If Someone Like Yourself From
> The Family Could Come And Help. It Would Not Take Long To
> Get Everything Straightened Out. I Would Have Been Out Yester-
> day If I Had An Attorney. Timothy, <u>I Need Help Badly</u>!*

He gave me the names and phone numbers of a couple of women
from his church whom I could call to coordinate our efforts. In a
postscript he wrote: "I Started 9 Books Since Inside Writing 15/20
Pages Daily. Need To Ask You Info. On Publishing, Etc."

My mother was appalled when she learned I'd been in contact
with Lee. "Tim," she told me, "*do not try to help your uncle.*" This
was the same tone of voice she'd use to tell me not to go near a

hot burner when I was a child. "It's very compassionate of you to want to try to help him, that's a good quality, write him letters if you want, but *do not* get involved with his life. He is just . . . *so* crazy—your father and I tried to protect you from his craziness, and I guess we did too good a job of it, because you just don't know how crazy he is. Believe me—he will make *you* crazy trying to help him." Mom still tells the story of how I put my hand on a hot burner even after she'd told me not to.

I think I tried to help my uncle not because my father would've wanted me to—in fact he would likely have forbidden it—but because it's what he would've done himself. My mother, in explaining why she'd never remarried, once called my father "a hard act to follow." Even among my friends, "Walt," as everyone but me called him, had had an image as a supremely capable fellow who'd appear in a crisis and fix everything with brisk élan. Once, years after my father's death, a friend of mine was complaining at a party about painful periodontal problems he couldn't afford to get fixed, and, before considering whether there might be a better time to make the offer, I blurted out, "Jesus, *I'll* pay for it. You can pay me back whenever. Just get them fixed!" I was embarrassed to have made such a thoughtless show of magnanimity in front of a group, but he later told me, "It was very Walt-like." Trying to help Uncle Lee made me feel grown-up and competent, more like my father.

None of which I particularly was. When I phoned one of the women Lee had referred me to, one Rhonda Rawlins, I got some inkling of what my father must have been dealing with his whole life. Rhonda and her friend Amanda sounded pitifully relieved that at last A Man had stepped in to take over. "We don't understand these things," they kept whining. "We're just women." I had never before spoken to any female who unabashedly offered up her gender as an excuse for ignorance or incompetence. But this, of course, is exactly the kind of person who would be gulled by Uncle

Lee's charms. I had begun this call by jotting down some practical information, names and phone numbers, in the manner of my father's lists, but at some point during the conversation I stopped taking any notes at all and started doodling little horrified Munchlike faces and writing things like "IDIOTS," "NIGHTMARE," and "<u>DON'T GO</u>."

Needless to say, everything did not get quickly straightened out. "Not Good, Tim," Lee wrote me the day of his verdict. "The Jury Found Me Guilty Of All Charges After Five Hours Of Deliberation. Kind Of Hard To Believe Since I'm Not Guilty Of Any Of The Charges." It was, indeed, hard to believe. He still maintained that he was being persecuted because he had dared to challenge shadowy, powerful political interests: "I Found Out The Hard Way These Good Old Boys Do Hang Tight. To Run Against One Of Them Is An <u>Absolute</u> No-No."

A year after his conviction, my girlfriend Margot and I took a road trip to Florida whose ultimate purpose was to visit Uncle Lee in jail. As a present for him I took along a small plant that takes all its nourishment from the air—an epiphyte. This one was nestled in a shell, its green tendrils protruding like the stalks and claws of a hermit crab. This had been Margot's suggestion. It was a small living thing he could keep in his cell that required neither soil nor water, something that could thrive in a crevice of cement. It also seemed to me that Lee was not unlike an epiphyte himself— rootless, subsisting in the most improbable niches, apparently living on nothing at all. In between going to beaches and Gatorland and Medieval Times I spent much of that week on pay phones with prison officials, trying to set up a visit. I became acquainted with the stupidity and obstructionism, intractable literal-mindedness, and Uroboric logic of the penal system.

The day Margot and I arrived at the correctional facility for my scheduled visit, I was told that the night before my uncle had been transferred to the prison hospital, where visitors weren't allowed.

I spent an hour and a half in a small cinder-block room explaining through wire-mesh reinforced glass and a speakerphone that I'd driven here all the way from Maryland and had to head back that same day. I was told that they understood that. Calls were placed as far up in the state correctional hierarchy as they could go on a weekend, but the final, considered answer was the same as the initial, reflexive one: no. The explanation I was given over and over was that the prison hospital simply wasn't set up for visitors. A prison system treats everyone like a prisoner, regarded as suspect, subject to arbitrary rules and unappealable decisions. I finally gave up and reported wearily back to Margot outside, knowing that I faced yet another hopeless circular argument with her: what had they said, what did *I* say, had I explained this, had I tried that. There is a photograph of me, wearing sunglasses and a dress shirt tucked into blue jeans, arms spread in a gesture of impotence, my hair blown into my face by the wind, standing in front of the unscenic backdrop of an electrified fence, the low slit-windowed prison building, and, beyond it, the cooling towers of a nuclear plant. Looking at this photo recently, Margot recalled, "I was weeping with rage as I took this." I had reached the limits of my helpfulness.

I am, obviously, not my father. The ways in which I'm best able to help people are silly and impractical ones. I've also had enough experience with the mentally ill and addicted to know that the people in most desperate need of help are often the most adamantly unhelpable. Not only will you fail to help them, but they will deplete every bit of help you have—your money, time, patience, and kindness—and then move on to the next pushover as unthinkingly as a swarm of locusts devouring a field. These days mental illness seems about as fascinating to me as colon cancer. The last friendship I severed was with someone who was, like Lee, bipolar, and an addict. When a schizophrenic artist I admire called me up recently to confront me over some delusional

betrayal, I told him clearly and evenly that I was not going to engage with him, and hung up. Every once in a while I'll still get a
cryptic text from an unknown number that reads like an in-joke,
except I'm not in on it, and I'll know that some former friend has
gone off his meds again. I know better by now than to reply, but
sometimes I still do.

After my failed visit, I corresponded with Uncle Lee only inter-
mittently. He became more and more preoccupied with his dete-
riorating health. "I'm Beginning To Think Of [the prison doctor]
As The Grim Reaper As She Consistently Wears Black Skirt &
Shoes. . . ." He was also fixated on the fantasy of an early condi-
tional medical release. In May 1997 he wrote me a jubilant letter
instructing me to rent out his old P.O. box in Granite Cliffs—Box
#1000. He was willing to offer one hundred dollars to the present
occupant to get it if it was already taken.

> *I Should Be Released Yet This Month From Prison And Will Re-*
> *port To County Parole & Probation—After That I Intend To Fly*
> *Into Phila. Int. Airport Having Floyds* [my aunt's family] *Pick Me*
> *Up. I Will Rent Or Buy A Car Or Pick-Up To Come To Port De-*
> *posit To Pick Up Mail & Rent While I Confer With J.H.U. Hospital*
> *RE: Feasibility Of Dual (Heart/Kidney) Transplant & Prostratec-*
> *tomy. . . . My Paramour Rhonda May Be Riding "Shotgun" With*
> *Me As Well.*

His letter was pure manic delusion, of course. No medical release was imminent. His official release date was not until April
11, 2006, which he would not live to see. But the letter effectively
called my bluff. For all my professed sympathy for his plight, I
had to admit to myself that I had no actual wish to see my uncle
Lee get out of jail. Granite Cliffs, the town where he intended to
rent out his P.O. box, was only ten minutes from where I lived. I
was, frankly, afraid that he would show up any day, wanting to

sleep on my couch, borrow money, drive my car on the beach. He would forge my signature on checks and deeds and loan applications, stick me with all the bills, burn down my house.

A month later I received an envelope with lettering even more flamboyantly crazy than usual—capitals like the imaginary letters in Dr. Seuss's *On Beyond Zebra!*, with flourishes like barbed devil's tails. The envelope was scrawled with warnings: "Legal Mail/ Privileged Mail/Dated Mail." Enclosed was a Xerox copy of a letter from my aunt Lynn, my father and Lee's sister, anxiously inquiring about Lee's status—she'd heard he was refusing his psych medication and was under suicide watch. At the bottom of this, Lee had written:

> *Please Call* The *Attorney General Of U.S.A.!, Immediately! I Am Being Beaten Into Submission, Improperly (Intentionally) Medicated, & My Heart & Kidneys Are In Failure. My Prostate Has Cancer.*

Beneath that was something else, written in such a febrile hand I had to squint to make it out:

> *Captain Slater Is Burying Beaten Dead Convicts Near Here Somewhere.*

I stopped writing back.

My ex-girlfriend Margot, who went on to take an entire family of Laotian refugees into her home for years, is dubious about our ability to help anyone. She tends to think the sanest policy is a sort of spiritual triage, saving your efforts for those who are likely to make it with a little immediate aid—a small loan, a job recommendation, a couch to crash on for a week or two—and dispassionately ignoring the moribund. But what do you do if you don't have the option to walk away, to hang up or hit IGNORE, because you're bound to someone by obligation or love? What if he's your brother? What if your elderly mother, whose letters are mostly preoccupied with her gardening, thanks you for looking after him?

My father's compromise was to keep his brother so effectively compartmentalized from the rest of his family that we were barely aware he existed. He understood that his brother was not responsible—meaning dangerous as well as blameless—and believed that he belonged under psychiatric supervision for life. Whether he did Lee, or society, any favors by helping him avoid a life sentence in jail is debatable. In the end Lee frustrated my father's best efforts to help him. But he never stopped trying, in the few diminishing ways he could. The last testaments to his devotion are receipts for little conveniences he bought for his brother in prison, subscriptions to newspapers and magazines, and yellowing ads for a JCPenney clock radio ($29.95) and headphone set ($9.95) circled in fading black Flair pen.

The last time he ever wrote me, Lee mused, "I Wonder What Walt Would Say If I Told Him I'd Been Locked Up Down in Redneck Northern Florida For Nearly Eight Years And Not Seen A Kreider Yet Much Less So Much As A Letter." His brother had finally become his benefactor in memory. At one point Lee sent me a will, which was never notarized or witnessed and probably would have been invalidated on the basis of the handwriting alone. It named me as executor, bequeathed all his earthly belongings to the Billy Graham Evangelistic Campaign, and included a design for his gravestone. When Lee died of heart failure in 2003 his body was cremated, and as far as I know he has no grave. The marker he imagined for himself was to have had an oval space for a photo and bore the inscription, "Farmer in Nature, Seaman at Heart." The base was to be quarried from Granite Cliffs, he specified, and the headpiece carved of old white marble—"Like <u>Walt's</u>."

My mother's voice still tightens with old sorrow and anger when she talks about Lee. She says it makes her stomach clench just to think about him. I was kept so successfully insulated from him for so long that at first this seemed to me like an overreaction. The man's been dead for almost a decade. But then she reluctantly told me about some of the grotesque accusations he'd made against my father from prison in the last years of his life, and that he'd threatened not only to sue but to kill—I believe the legal term is *murder*—members of our family. I lay awake that night feeling not so much threatened as sullied, molested, by my uncle Lee's scummy lies and jailhouse threats, the way you'd feel if you'd accidentally seen child pornography or a snuff film. Once you let people like my uncle into your head they will do as much damage as they can, like intruders trashing your home out of spite. I understood now why my mother was still afraid of this man, even though he was a can of ashes now.

I can understand why people once believed in vampires and dybbuks, demons who took the guises of loved ones. One of the cruelest aspects of mental illness is that those afflicted become indistinguishable from their affliction; they are possessed by it. I know people who've had relatives whose personalities changed after strokes or head injuries, but they, at least, could tell themselves that this wasn't their grandfather—their "real" grandfather was the person he'd been before the trauma. But my uncle started exhibiting criminal behavior in his teens. It's impossible to know what kind of person he would've been if he hadn't been sick; there is no Platonic ideal of Lee, untouched by madness, to whom we can compare the sad reality of his lifelong self. One of the most pitiable things about John Merrick, the "Elephant Man," was his undisfigured arm—"a delicately shaped limb covered with fine skin and provided with a beautiful hand which any woman might have

envied"—a glimpse of the man he was meant to be, all but smoth-
ered inside the aspect of a monster. The only glimpse I ever got of
this man in my uncle—of any capacity for self-awareness, candor,
or humor—was when I asked him about that bankbook I'd found.
He never acknowledged my question, but he signed his next letter:
"Your Uncle, Lorenzo von Kreidler."

Chutes and Candyland

Several years ago I was sitting at a bar in Cripple Creek, Colorado, that had video poker games built right into the bartop when a promo came on TV for the upcoming *Oprah*. That afternoon's episode was to feature an interview with Jennifer Finney Boylan, a novelist who was promoting a new memoir about her male-to-female sex change.

"Hey," I said out loud. "I *know* her." This is not the sort of thing I would ordinarily blurt out in an unfamiliar bar, but it's not every day you see someone you know on *Oprah*. Maybe the beer was making me chatty. I would learn in a few hours that I was suffering from altitude sickness.

The guy next to me, who was wearing a hat with a rooster feather stuck in the band and a bolo tie, studied the screen, absorbing the gist of the episode.

"So was that," he asked, groping diplomatically for the mot juste, "weird?"

I said: "Yes." He just nodded. We both sipped our beers.

I met Jim Boylan twenty-five years ago, when I was assigned to be his teaching assistant at a summer writing program for kids, where, for easily defensible pedagogical reasons, we blindfolded fourteen-year-old girls and then fed them hummingbird nectar and made them touch an inflatable Godzilla. Jim was a graduate student at the university where I was an undergrad, and after that summer, instead of taking, say, a course on *Ulysses* with one of the world's foremost Joyce scholars, I kept signing up for Jim's classes, which had titles like "Comedy and Horror" and "Modernism, Metafiction, and Irrealism." (We never got around to covering whatever "Irrealism" was.) He'd always host the last class at his off-campus apartment, one of which symposia ended with three aspiring fictionists setting off fireworks in a pie in a park across the street. Once in a while I'd stop by and visit him at home, where he'd play songs of his own composition, like "Mister Rogers Does the Puppets' Voices," on the autoharp, or we'd play a round of Chutes and Candyland, a paradigm-shifting game of our own invention.

Jim was what they call a Male Role Model for me, much as that may sound like a straight line now. He was the first person I personally knew to have a book published, even if it was with a university press and had a lurid purple and turquoise cover. It made getting into print seem like something that might happen to a real person. I acquired from him a taste for Juicy Juice, a children's beverage with surprising cross-generational appeal. He introduced me to music whose genre I could not even identify, like the Penguin Café Orchestra. I remember listening to what he had to say to someone who was chronically ill, taking mental notes on how to be kind in such a situation. For a while my laugh even started sounding like his—I was at an age when the tics and mannerisms of people we admire are as infectious as chicken pox among toddlers. His laugh was a high, snickering thing, unmistakable—I remember being in a darkened auditorium and realizing, as the entire audience laughed at a line, that Jim was in attendance. His father died of cancer around the same time that my own father was diagnosed. I don't remember his presuming to offer me any advice about this, but, as with getting published, knowing it had happened to Jim made it seem real.

After college, I'd visit him and his wife once a year at his new home in Maine, during the Perseid meteor showers in the first week of August. During this time we would regress together into a couple of ten-year-old spazzes. The high point of one year's visit was seeing a little girl vomit at at least a couple of *g*'s on a ride called the Skymaster at the Skowhegan State Fair, a scene we immortalized in both song and ritual reenactment. There was an activity called Naked Fireworks. One year we pulled over at a yard sale and purchased some large plush animals: a dog in lederhosen and a Tyrolean hat, whom we named Frïtzl, and a sad, understuffed rabbit we called Mister Lucky. Frïtzl we threw off a bridge with a cinder block tied to his paw. We strung up Mister Lucky on a mountaintop with a sign hung around his neck that said: A LYIN', THIEVIN', LETTUCE-RUSTLIN' VARMINT.

But those visits weren't just about puerile high spirits; they were mountaintop retreats for me, where I could breathe in some clear air and take a longer view before returning to the messy trenches of my own life, where I was still drawing minicomics in front of a space heater with the TV on, miserably trying to figuring out what I was supposed to be. From Jim's hot tub, where we'd sip whiskey watching the Perseids leave their incandescent trails across the sky like afterimages on the retina, the densely clustered stars of the Maine night looked vertiginously three-dimensional; I felt not as if I were on top of the earth looking up, but stuck on the outside of the planet looking out into the galaxy around us. The week after my father's funeral, sitting with Jim in a boat in the middle of Long Pond in the rippling light of August, I said out loud, to my own surprise: "Life could not be pleasanter." One night that same week, before Jim went up to bed, out of nowhere he said to me, "Good night, Timbo," something no one but my father had ever called me. He played songs on the piano with a wistful, yearning tenor, chords I could never seem to find at home. There was some music I could only ever hear at Jim's house.

I understand now that a lot of what I felt on those trips was the ache that young adults, still unformed and adrift and very much aware of it, feel on looking at someone who's far enough ahead of them on life's timeline to seem more settled in the world and at peace with themselves, but still close enough to beckon them on and call back, *See, it's not so bad up here, keep going, you'll be fine.* Whether they're happy or not they are, at least, content. They've made their choices and learned to live with them. They have, for better or worse, become themselves.

Which is one reason it shook me so personally when Jim announced that he was neither happy nor content—nor had he ever truly been himself. What he was, it turned out, was transgendered. "You know," he wrote me, "the whole woman-trapped-in-a-man's-body thing."

Jim came out to me in a long letter sent after the Perseids had come and gone in the summer of 2000; I'd known something was amiss with the Boylans for some time, because Jim had put off my usual yearly visit the summer before, telling me that he and his wife were having some serious summit talks, reassuring me only that no one was gay, getting divorced, or had cancer. This was not among the possibilities I'd considered. "Having read this far, you're probably thinking something along the lines of 'what the fuck,'" he wrote. "That's exactly what I've always thought about it, in fact." He went on to tell me about a whole life he'd been living unknown to me or anyone else: how he'd dreamed of himself as female from earliest childhood, furtively cross-dressed in high school and college, and secretly ventured out into the Baltimore night dressed as a woman in grad school, when I'd known him. After years of trying to ignore it, hoping that he might be made normal by marriage or parenthood, he'd finally admitted to himself, at age forty, that he could not go on living the way he'd lived his whole life. He'd come out to his wife, who was a social worker and about as well prepared to understand his condition as anyone could be. He was currently undergoing hormone therapy and was planning to transition into being a woman full-time. He reassured me that my friendship was a crucial one to him and hoped that we would be able to talk the whole weird thing out somehow. After his(/her?)* signature—an ambiguous *J*—s/he appended a crude, childish doodle like two inverted fermata, captioned: "My buzums." This, at least, seemed to augur well for some continuity in our friendship.

My girlfriend, arriving for dinner that night, found me sitting on my porch steps where I'd read the letter, holding my head in my hands as though it required constant firm external pressure to keep it intact. Talk about Chutes and Candyland: I felt as though I had suddenly slid into another game altogether, with a completely different set of rules. I now had to thoroughly re-understand someone I'd thought I'd known for ten years. It was retroactively shocking to realize that at any one of those times when I'd casually dropped in unannounced on Jim in Baltimore I might've caught him playing the autoharp in a skirt. I could hardly stand to think of the years of secrecy and isolation he'd endured—sitting alone in his apartment with the blinds drawn, grading our papers on Borges in drag, all dressed up with no place to go. It was hard to imagine the gut-clenching dread and hope you'd feel and the bravery it would take to make your fingers let go of a letter like the one I'd just read and commend it to the mailbox.

My first response was to phone Jim—Jenny?—and reassure him—*her*—that although the news had indeed come as something of a shock and I intended to write her a long letter in reply, I would always be her friend, and we'd figure it all out. Which was, of course, just what I was supposed to say. Not that I didn't

---

* Pronoun trouble noted but insoluble. This will only get worse before it gets better.

mean it; just that, having said all the right things, actually doing them was a different matter. There was, I think, an inverse relationship between how close people were to Jim and their readiness to accept his new identity. It's easy to demonstrate how progressive and open-minded and loyal you are when it costs you nothing. Jim worked at a New England liberal arts college, where acceptance of her transition was not only the appropriate social reaction but mandatory under the university's official diversity policy. His colleagues and acquaintances accepted her new identity as a matter of political correctness, professional protocol, and the traditional Yankee policy of minding one's own business. They changed the *Jim*s to *Jenny*s and *he*s to *she*s in the same way that they'd learned to say *Asian* instead of *Oriental* sometime in the nineties. But for those of us who'd loved Jim for years, and thought we'd known him, it was more complicated.

Historically, I had not adapted easily to change. When an ex-girlfriend of mine, who'd gone by the nickname Sandi the whole time we dated, later reverted to her actual name, Margot, it took me years of mental translation to adjust. I think of her as Margot now, but if you were to ask me whether I'd ever dated a Margot I'd say no. Pronouns are ground even deeper into our brains; *he* and *she* are so automatic that suddenly switching them is like having to learn to drive on the other side of the road. Jenny was forgiving of the inevitable slipups at first, but if they persisted you could tell it got on her nerves. (She went so far as to threaten a colleague of hers, who could not seem to bother to make much effort to change, with a formal complaint.) Even within the last year I once referred to Jenny as "him" in front of her in a bar. It made me wince in the same way you would if you accidentally called your spouse by someone else's name. There's no backpedaling or covering or explaining it away; you've involuntarily revealed some impolitic truth, the kind that means you're going to have to have a Conversation. From her closest friends, Jenny was asking for a deeper, more genuine acceptance than the acquiescence to forms of address that political correctness calls "respect." She didn't want to be humored; she wanted to be taken seriously. She wanted us to think of her, truly, as a woman.

Which was impossible. I had known Jim Boylan for ten years. There was no way I would ever think of Jenny as a woman as automatically and unconsciously as I think of my friends Annie or Lauren or Lucy as women. But just because it may have been an unrealistic wish didn't mean it was an unreasonable one. To Jenny, who had thought of herself as female since before she could talk, it seemed that she was asking for a kind of respect so basic that most of us don't think of it as respect at all, only simple recognition. It's the same sort of privilege whereby white people seldom have to think of themselves as white—just as people. Her only real wish, throughout her transition, was that others should see her as the person she felt herself to be—which wish is shared by everyone, and is, of course, granted none of us.

Some of my acquaintances were surprisingly intolerant about Jenny's transition. One of them likened transsexuals to people with a paraphilia for auto-amputation. ("I never felt like a whole person as long as I had two legs," is how one such case memorably put it.) This seemed not just unsympathetic but a bad analogy; renouncing your status as a tetrapod is pretty straightforward pathology, but gender has never been as unambiguously binary as people like to pretend. There's also a high correlation between gender identity disorder in males and prenatal exposure to diethylstilbestrol (DES), a synthetic estrogen that was given to pregnant women to prevent miscarriage from the 1940s through the '70s, including Jim's mother. And, asking myself whether Jim seemed delusional in any other area, I concluded that he did not. Although there are plenty of people who are sane and reasonable in all matters except for the one pet subject on which you do not want to get them started, Jim didn't sound irrational when he talked about his condition; he knew how bizarre it was, he'd been baffled and embarrassed by it his whole life, and he was all too aware of what he might be forfeiting by trying to integrate it into the rest of his life.

But I still found myself groping for some analogy to that condition, something more familiar: was it as if Jim were gay, and coming out of the closet? Like he was confessing to an affair, the kind of hopeless, inappropriate love that tears your life in two? Or was it more like fibromyalgia or lupus, some medical problem I just didn't know much about? Had Jim Boylan died? Who *was* Jenny Boylan? The only instructive model I could find anywhere in art or literature was an episode of *Star Trek*. Maybe my mistake was in trying to find an analogy at all; there simply was no precedent for this in my own experience. But then I'd never had situs inversus or seen a ghost or been to the Moon, either; that didn't necessarily mean no one else ever had. I finally accepted that I was going to have to file this under Things I'm Never Going to Understand, a mental file already crammed to overflowing.

What I could relate to was the common fear that you are secretly so uniquely screwed-up that there is no way anyone would like you if they really knew you. In an old short story of Jim's, he had described a character who bore an obvious physical resemblance to himself from a woman's point of view by saying: "There was something charming, yet also slightly unpleasant, something false, about him. Like he was nice enough in general but used his articulateness as a means of covering up the fact that he collected worms or something."[1] Now the Worm Museum was open to the public.

One of the more inappropriate emotions I encountered in grappling with Jenny's transition was a kind of envy. Of course I didn't envy Jim the years of secrecy and shame he had endured, or what more he would have to undergo, and risk losing, to become who he wanted to be. I knew how lethal secrets can be, and I was proud of Jim for dragging his into the light instead of letting it devour him.

But I had always sensed in Jim some of the same sadness that inhabited me—it was a bond between us deeper than our goofball hijinks or our love of literature, the thing that lay beneath them both. It was a kind of brotherhood. And I'd assumed that he was sad for the same reason I was: having to be a person in the world. Most of the people I loved were outsiders and misfits, skulking around on the margins, their fundamental relationship to the world one of being misplaced. Once, after watching me play a piano piece using my own idiosyncratic self-taught technique, which, like my typing, doesn't use the pinkies at all, Jim said: "You're weirder than me." His tone was funny—like a legless beggar checking out the new guy on his block who's just a torso. So it was jarring to learn that Jim's sadness had always been something so much stranger and more specific than my own. And that his could be fixed. I couldn't help but wonder, in a selfish, petulant way: so what operation do *I* get? I suppose I felt the way some lesbians must when one of their number suddenly ups and marries a man, defects to conventionality. Not just abandoned but betrayed, as if one of a besieged cadre had deserted.

Jenny would argue that she'd never been a man; she'd just been impersonating one. I would say, *You and me both.* That's what we're all doing—trying, with varying degrees of success, to impersonate our assigned genders. This life is like a costume party where we all get handed an arbitrary outfit at the door and told, *Here, you're a pirate.* If you say *But I wanted to be a princess* they say, *Tough—we got enough princesses already, you're a pirate,* so you put on your eye patch and hook and fake parrot and wander around halfheartedly waving your cutlass saying *Arrrr—Aye'm a purr-ty princess!,* feeling ridiculous and wretched. Even now, whenever I change a tire or throw a football with a respectable spiral, I'm still secretly impressed by my own display of male competence. There's always a sense of successful fraudulence to it, the way you feel the first time you manage to order food or ask directions in a foreign language.

Jenny's condition was not comparable to my own discomfort with the dumb cultural codes of gender. What I experienced metaphorically was for her painfully literal, physical; it was like the difference between having a cancer of the soul and cancer of the pancreas. For Jenny's own account of her transition you can read her eloquent and funny memoir, *She's Not There: A Life in Two Genders;* it's the closest most of us will come to understanding what it's like to be transgendered. But her transition also inadvertently illuminated some of my own comfortably unexamined assumptions about gender and sex and identity by testing them to their limits, just as it's in black holes, those places where the laws of physics break down in extremis, that we glean new insights into the most fundamental structure of nature.

We are all unavoidably ignorant about the experience of the opposite sex; it might be easier for me to imagine growing up in a Paleolithic tribe in Papua New Guinea than it is to imagine growing up as a girl in my own hometown. I do know that we both have to endure a crushing amount of indoctrination into our respective genders. I remember a childhood friend of mine telling me not to sit with my legs crossed, because men didn't sit like that. (This was the same kid who instructed me that *toilet* was pronounced *terlet.*) I thought, *My dad sits like that,* but I also uncrossed my legs. This mostly unspoken code only got more rigid and intricate and harshly enforced in adolescence. My sister complained, in middle school, that her formerly intelligent friends were suddenly acting giggly and dumb because boys liked them better that way. Some of the rules verged on superstitions of the Babylonian dog-on-the-bed variety: boys could not carry their books clasped to their chests but had to lug them all under one arm, no matter how unwieldy a stack they had; if you wore an earring in your right ear it meant you were gay; if you wore green on a Thursday you were gay.

It didn't end in adulthood, although the code is less crudely enforced than in middle school. My female friends who don't shave their legs describe it as by far the most transgressive thing they do; they report getting nasty looks from other women as though it were an act of gender betrayal, outing them all as hairy creatures hardly less repulsive than men. Last winter I wore a very silly knit polar-bear-head hat that endeared me to women and children, but men often gave it and me contemptuous looks, as if the hat brought discredit upon us all. It had little ears. I don't know, maybe it's just a stupid hat. My own mother told me it made me look like a lunatic.

Jenny had to go through this socialization ordeal twice—once, in childhood and adolescence, learning how to act like a male, and again in middle age, learning how to act like a female. She had warned me that this second adolescence could be, not unlike the first one, a little insufferable for bystanders. She was going to be allowed to be female for the first time, and so was as excited about, and inexpert with, fashion and cosmetics as a fourteen-year-old girl. When I saw she'd captioned a photo of herself on her website "Skirt by Coldwater Creek," I felt she had crossed over into some truly alien country. It wasn't my friend wearing a skirt that disturbed me; it was my friend *caring* about skirts. For the first time I wondered: *Who* is *this person?*

She took lessons with a voice coach to refine her feminine voice. At first it sounded too Valley Girlish in its inflections, with a bit of that ditzy interrogative lilt at the ends of sentences. I'm not sure whether I even would've noticed it coming from someone I'd always known as female, but coming from my old friend Jim, it initially creeped me out like the voice of a split-personality ventriloquist in a movie. I think this initial Valley Girl phase was an overcompensation—I can only imagine how self-conscious and scared she must've been using it in public at first, like venturing out into the night in women's clothes back in grad school, hoping to pass. Over time, though, it's evened out to the point where I can no longer remember how Jim used to sound any different.

The first photos Jenny sent me of herself as a woman gave me the willies. I was experiencing the gender equivalent of what psychologists call the Uncanny Valley, whereby something looks a little too real, but not quite real enough, for comfort, like low-budget CGIs. To my eye, it was not quite Jim anymore, and yet still too much him to look like somebody else. It was like the vase-and-faces illusion, positive and negative space reversing to yield two entirely different images. I had this same disorienting experience when I first met Jenny in person, for drinks at the Algonquin Hotel. At times it felt perfectly natural, sitting in a hotel lobby chatting with a female friend, but then at moments I'd get what felt like the first panicky wave of onrushing LSD and realize I was sitting in public with Jim Boylan in drag. It was irreal! Jenny was drinking some flagrantly girly cocktail in a secondary color, garnished with fruit and a swizzle stick. I ordered a large glass of gin.

I have no idea how Jenny looks to other people—whether, as the transgendered say, they ever "read" her as male. I *think* she looks like a tall, striking soccer mom with long ash-blond hair. (Once I was describing her to someone in these terms and a guy at the end of the bar roused himself from a stupor to holler, "I'll take her on spec!") My female friends who've known her only as a woman can't imagine her ever having been a man. Looking back at old photos of Jim now, it's hard for me to articulate exactly how Jenny looks different from him. The superficials are nearly identical; the difference is something essential.

I also can't tell whether Jim's old personality has changed or whether other people's perceptions of him/her have. Some of my friends thought she was extremely competitive with me, which would probably have gone unremarked-upon between male friends, and is hardly unheard-of among artists of either gender. Some people—most of them female—found Jenny self-absorbed, talking incessantly about herself. I don't recall anyone making this criticism of Jim, even though he was also very much a center-of-attention kind of guy, the sort who clowns and holds forth as a way of drowning out his fundamental discomfort with himself. I'm not certain whether Jenny finds herself more interesting and worth talking about since the sex change—it is, after all, a pretty un-one-uppable conversational topic—or if she's just more at ease with herself. It's also possible that people read the same personality traits s/he's always had very differently now that she's female. We expect men to be loud and funny and talk about themselves; we think of these guys as big personalities, boisterous and fun. It's not always charming, but it's also not unacceptable. When Jenny acts this way I think it seems, to other women, as if she's cheating, getting to have it both ways. Girls are taught to listen, ask questions, and laugh at men's jokes; a woman who makes herself the focus risks being seen as vain, obnoxious, needy, or insecure—as *unattractive*.

It was hard to know how much I was now seeing her through my own preconceptions about women. Our relationship was changing for other reasons—as we both got older the age difference between us no longer mattered as much, and I was finding my own odd, meandering path as an artist—so it was impossible to parse out how much of it had to do with her transition. A few months after she'd started on hormone therapy, Jenny wrote me an earnest letter expressing concern about my life. For the first time in our decade of friendship, she told me she sometimes worried about my apparent aimlessness and short-term, immediate-reward, regret-minimization philosophy. She wondered whether it might not lend my days some structure, and make my life more meaningful, if I were to do something for others, maybe volunteer work or teaching—something, yes, perhaps not unlike like a job. I wrote her: "Wow—that estrogen works fast."

I grew up in the 1970s, when it was not just intellectually fashionable but, in some circles, politically mandatory to believe that all gender differences were culturally conditioned. (This idea has been somewhat qualified over the last few decades by genetic and evolutionary explanations for human behavior, and by that generation's own experience of raising kids.) At the same time that we grade schoolers were being taught that the color green was gay on Thursdays, this conscientious gender blindness was filtering down to us through the medium of Norman Lear sitcoms and girls-can-do-anything-boys-can cartoon agitprop. As an adult, I think of myself as a pretty gender-indifferent guy: I have as many close female friends as male, and none of them are what you'd call girly girls—they're all unabashedly intelligent, funny, and assertive, in flagrant defiance of middle-school norms. None of them reads checkout-aisle fashion magazines, not even as a "guilty pleasure." They do seem to think about shoes more than I do. My male friends, even the ex-marines, rocket scientists, and hunters who've shot six-hundred-pound boars, are all pretty gentle, sensitive guys who don't need to get blacked-out drunk to talk about their relationship troubles or admit that they enjoy each other's company. None of them gives a shit about cars. Some of them do get excited about professional football, but this I regard as a regrettable genetic defect, like the predisposition toward sickle-cell anemia among African-Americans. I tend to think that anyone who conforms too closely to his or her assigned gender role must not be all that independent-minded or brave.

Acting any differently toward women than I did around men—even just softening my voice when I talked to them—made me feel faintly calculating and fake. It was the same kind of shame I felt if I caught myself dropping g's around black people or lowering my diction with mechanics or repairmen—or, for that matter, feeling more confident around girls I wasn't attracted to. In retrospect it's obvious I was confusing a lot of different issues and making myself crazy second-guessing pretty common and innocuous behavior. But when Jenny came out to me, I was still clinging half-consciously to some belief that I treated people entirely on the basis of their individual personalities rather than incidentals like gender. So when one of my closest guy friends unexpectedly switched sexes, it called me on my bullshit.

Think, for a moment, just about how you'd act toward a female friend who's in the hospital versus the way you would toward a man in the same situation. I, for one, feel freer to be tender and solicitous toward a woman who's sick or injured. With a man there's a little more joshing and shoulder punching, concern disguised as its opposite. When my friend Kevin was about to go in for an angioplasty we had a conversation about whether his friends would be allowed to eat him if he died. All this goes back to our earliest experiences of being comforted as children when we bang our heads or skin our knees: girls are fawned and cooed over and kissed to make it better, boys told to stop crying now and act like a big boy.

I got the opportunity to test this *gedankenexperiment* in real life when Jenny asked me if I would travel to Neenah, Wisconsin, for nine days to keep her company through her convalescence from what's formally called "gender reassignment" surgery. My policy has always been, when someone asks you if you will travel to Wisconsin to nurse them through sex change surgery, to say yes.

There wasn't much that wasn't irreal about my time in Neenah. Jenny's surgeon had the implausible mad-scientist name of Dr. Schrang. A Schrang, Jenny assured me, was the Cadillac of vaginas: "sensate, mucosal, and orgasmic." Jenny shared a room with a transgendered woman from Virginia whose family occasionally phoned to remind her that she was a freak and an abomination in the eyes of the Lord. Several times a day Jenny had to insert a stent, an object not unlike a dildo, into her new vagina, to keep it from closing. She named her stents after recent Democratic presidents of the United States, ranging in size from Jimmy Carter, the starter model, to the formidable Lyndon Baines Johnson. During this procedure I would usually go for walks around the hospital corridors. Patients recovering from gender reassignment shared a floor with the cardiac ward, and my perceptions of gender had by this time become so thoroughly unmoored that I would see a grizzled, gray-faced man with a sagging belly in a hospital gown making his way laboriously down the hall with a walker and think, *I hope that guy had a heart attack*. Ever since Neenah, the efforts of would-be subversive persons at "gender-bending" have left me feeling less fucked with or challenged than condescended to, like a veteran getting mugged by some punk.

One little test of my mettle came when Jenny, who turned out to be allergic to hydrocodone, broke out into shingles and asked me to rub moisturizer on her back. Obviously I realized this was a nonsexual request, strictly a medicinal procedure, except a man probably wouldn't ask another man to do it for him. What do you do when a friend of yours, formerly a male friend but now a female, asks you to rub lotion on her back? "My heterosexuality is hanging by a thread," I mostly mock-lamented, smearing the lotion into her red scaly skin, while she laughed her same old snickering laugh in triumph. I appropriated the rest of the hydrocodone as compensation.

It should be pointed out that, for someone who likes to pretend that that he treats men and women the same way, 100 percent of the people I've ever had sex with have been female. It's hard to believe that, if Jenny had always been a woman, we could've been friends for twenty-five years without sex ever at least presenting itself as a possibility. The only people who seem to believe in the phenomenon of men and women just being good friends all seem to have good friends who are pining miserably after them, waiting for them to break up with their significant others. Not to say that friendship between men and women is impossible, but there are few of these friendships in which sex doesn't at some point become an issue, if only to be acknowledged or dismissed.

The question of sex has since loomed into view on one or two occasions over the years—I'm remembering a harrowing episode when Jenny and I were more or less propositioned over shots of Jägermeister by a sailor and a woman claiming to be Cal Ripken Jr.'s niece—but the only time I ever addressed it directly was when Jenny, who'd been writing some freelance travel pieces, was offered the assignment to fly to Venice, and asked me whether I'd like to go along. I delicately tried to clarify whether we were talking about going to Venice or, you know, Going To Venice. I'd thought it was only taking her seriously as a woman to ask; if any other woman I knew had invited me to stay with her in one of the world's most legendarily romantic cities I would've made sure I understood the conditions before agreeing to go. Often such invitations are left deliberately ambiguous, but in this case I felt like I ought to err on the side of clarity. (Some of my trepidation may have dated back to a episode years earlier when I had traveled to Greece with a woman who, it turned out, had no intention of having sex with me, after which I declined an invitation to go to Italy with another woman who, in retrospect, pretty obviously did.) Jenny's reaction was: *It is so like a man to assume that going to Venice together would mean having sex.* I thought: *Only a woman could imagine that it didn't.* We never went to Venice.

But we'll always have Neenah. I had feared that my week there might be awkward, or at the very least boring, but I remember it now like one of our old summer vacation capers. We watched Buster Keaton comedies and Busby Berkeley musicals. Jenny illicitly split her Demerol with me and we washed it down with obscure midwestern beverages like Werner's Ginger Ale. And I read her *The Princess Bride* aloud. Reading to someone is an intimate thing to do; most of us have fond associations with being read to by our parents when we were children. The only other people I've read aloud to as an adult were girlfriends or my mother. Whenever anyone's tried reading to me I've fallen asleep within four pages,

still classically conditioned by bedtime stories. Jenny always snug-
gled down under the covers to listen with the cozy entitlement of
a favored daughter. She liked to yell "The Cliffs . . . of *Insanity!*"
whenever we came to this phrase in the book. She later described it
as "the girlhood she never had."

On our trip home from Neenah, Jenny hired a limousine to
drive us both from the Portland airport to her house in Maine.
There were three cassette tapes in the back of the limo; we chose
Yanni Live at the Acropolis. Jenny told me the story of the death of
her childhood cat Ba-Boing!, who was run over by the school bus
as young Jim and his sister watched in horror. Their mother made
them get on the bus and go to school and then rushed the cat to the
vet's, where she was asked, "What is this animal's name?" Holding
the cat's limp and flattened body in her arms, her face streaked with
tears, like a demented pietà, she had to answer: "Ba-Boing!" All this
told to the glittering synthetic crescendi of Yanni. This had always
happened to Jim and me—every time we got together we were reduced to the state of kids getting punchy at 3 a.m., unable to breathe,
feebly writhing, our faces red and wet and mushy with weeping.
(Did I mention that we still had plenty of leftover painkillers? Well,
we did.) Laughter is one of those intimacies, like orgasm or tears
or just getting completely snockered with someone, that bares our
most helpless, undignified selves. It's what's bound and consecrated
all my friendships, the way that sex consummates a love affair.

For a few years Jenny and I talked about what she called "the
ol' Presto Change-o" all the time, the same way we'd talked about
me getting stabbed quite a lot after that happened. But eventually
we ran out of things to say. She got her sex change and finally got
to be herself, and for a while she was euphoric, just as I'd been after
I didn't get killed and got to go on being me. But lately we talk a
lot more about the impossibility of knowing which of the things
you've done in life have really mattered, the sadness of seeing your
parents disengage from the business of living, the grotesque un-

fairness of getting old—the same insoluble problem of being a person in the world. The sex-change issue resolved itself the way most of life's most vexing problems do: not because I ever figured it out or came around to some conclusion, but because it simply got obviated, without my noticing it, by time and experience. I finally exhausted myself with all my efforts to divvy up and pin down and label and just gave up, the same way our chatterbox brains can be dumbstruck and freed by a koan. What is the sound of one hand clapping? *Ba-Boing!* It turned out I'd been asking the wrong question; it was never *is she a woman or is he a man,* but *what is a friend.*

I worry sometimes, such as when we're annoying an entire bar by playing Rock 'Em Sock 'Em Robots (a spirited game that unavoidably involves a lot of mechanical noise as well as some ritual shouting), that the extent to which I feel at ease around Jenny is a measure of my denial about anything having changed—that, on some level, I still think of her as One of the Guys, which is not exactly what any woman wants. But this sort of silly puerility is hardly limited to my male friendships: Annie and I are always conniving some illicit caper like leaving her ex's belongings piled on his porch or photographing her at the vacation home he never took her to, and my conversations with my ex-girlfriend Max revolve around topics like World War I flying aces and *The Count of Monte Cristo.** On one of our evenings in New York's East Village of drinking Belgian ale, eating chicken vindaloo, going to the Russian baths, and smoking cigars, Jenny pointed out to me: "You know, if you didn't know any better, you'd think I was a very interesting woman."

Jenny Boylan might be the one person in this world whom I now think of purely as a human being, free of all the corporeal baggage of chromosomes, hormones, and footwear. I certainly don't

---

* Max insists that we mostly talk about our feelings and food. Maybe what's significant here is that she remembers the feelings while I remember the flying aces.

think of her as a man anymore. It may be that I'll never think of her as a woman in quite the same way that I do my friends who were born as girls. But then I'm not sure the difference between my relationship with Jenny and these women is any greater than the difference between my relationship with Lauren, with whom I fell in and out of love and never so much as kissed, and my relationship with Lucy, both of us so well defended and fond of each other, always angling to connect across the gulf between us, or with Annie, who's like my evil twin sister. The longer you live, the more involuted and unique all your friendships become, until each is as exotic and alien from the others as creatures on widely divergent evolutionary branches, bearing as much resemblance to one another as a lightning whelk and a gnu.

An Insult to the Brain

In Which I Am Tasked with Reading
The Life and Opinions of Tristram Shandy, Gentleman
Aloud to My Mother, an Invalid

I'd failed twice to read *The Life and Opinions of Tristram Shandy, Gentleman.* It was my friend Harold who first urged me to read it, claiming it was his favorite book. He would quote allegedly hilarious lines like "Pray, my Dear, have you not forgot to wind up the clock?" and name-drop characters like Dr. Slop. I was dubious. Harold had read the thing in graduate school, where I suspected his boredom threshold had been unnaturally raised by a program of study designed to render the love of reading into something joyless enough to be respectable. I was sure that *Tristram Shandy* was a laugh riot compared to Henry James's *The Golden Bowl* (a title Harold still uttered like the name of a Vietnamese hamlet where his entire platoon had been wiped out), but I was having some trouble making it through the first chapter, which was just over one (1) page long.

I knew about *Tristram Shandy,* of course—anyone who studies English literature or writing at least hears about it. Everyone knows about the black page that represents death, the white page on which you are invited to draw your own ideal of feminine beauty rather than have Sterne describe his beloved. It's a nonlinear, stream-of-consciousness story, appropriating outside texts and nesting stories within stories—self-referential, metafictional, and postmodern two hundred years before anyone thought up names for those things. It deconstructs the novel at the same time it's inventing it. There are even little doodles. It sounds like fun!

I gave it another chance because of an aesthetic crush I developed on a bust of its author I found at the Metropolitan Museum of Art. This bust, carved from life by Joseph Nollekens, made Laurence Sterne look like the best person in the history of the world to be seated next to at a dinner party. The line where his marble lips met was perfectly straight, revealing nothing, but the subtle molding and shadow around one corner of the mouth gave it the quirk of an incipient smile. (German humorist Friedrich Nietzsche wrote of Sterne's prose: "The reader who demands to know . . . whether he is making a serious or a laughing face, must be given up for lost: for he knows how to encompass both in a *single* facial expression."[1]) He looked to me as if he were politely maintaining a straight face while mentally refining the devastating aside he was about to mutter out of the side of his mouth about whatever blowhard you were both stuck listening to. *That guy,* I told myself, *has got to be funny.*

This time I got bogged down somewhere around page 12. The eighteenth-century diction and elaborate circumlocutions were exhausting; I reread whole paragraphs and then had to re-reread them. Most of Sterne's satirical references to scholarly works and intellectual debates of his day were lost on me; by the time I'd flipped to the back of the book to read the endnote explaining the allusion it was a little too late to slay me. And its bawdy humor, which must've been very titillating indeed in the eighteenth century, consists mostly of arch double entendres involving puddings, very long noses, and nuns' "placket-holes." I was still carrying my copy around, pretending I hadn't given up on it yet, when my mother almost died.

e⁓

You know it's that phone call right away. It's the call you've always known was going to come someday but, you hoped—to use the same phrase your parents used long ago to reassure you about your own hypothetical death—*not for a very long time.* "Tim," began the message, "this is your brother-in-law." My sister's husband, a pediatrician, is an easy-to-like guy with whom I usually talk about things like Batman. Ordinarily he'd just say, "Hi, this is Scott." This was the first time I'd ever heard the voice he must use to deliver bad medical news—clear, direct, affectless. My mother was in the hospital, he told me. She'd collapsed at home, delirious, and been taken to the ER. My sister, who is also a doctor, was already at the hospital. When I called her, she told me that our mother was suffering from septic shock. Apparently she'd had a kidney stone, a calcite deposit the size of a sand grain that had caused a potentially lethal backup of toxins in her blood. She'd been found only by chance, by a county deputy she'd called earlier in the day for an unrelated reason. It had been, my sister said, "a rough night," which I understood to be the same kind of professional euphemism as "experiencing some discomfort." Mom was in an ICU now, on intravenous antibiotics, and we were waiting to see if the infection could be brought under control and the fever would break. "If I were talking to the relative of someone in Mom's condition," said my sister, "I would tell them to come."

Hospitals are like the landscapes in recurring dreams: forgotten as though they'd never existed in the interims between visits, but instantly familiar once you return. As if they've been there all along, waiting for you while you've been away. The endlessly branching corridors and circular nurses' stations all look identi-

cal, like some infinite labyrinth in a Borges story. It takes a day
or two to memorize the route from the lobby to your room. The
innocuous landscape paintings that seem to have been specifically
commissioned to leave no impression on the human brain are perversely seared into your long-term memory. You pass doorways
through which you can occasionally see a bunch of Mylar bal-
loons or a pair of pale, withered legs. Hospital beds are now just
as science fiction predicted, with the patient's vital signs digitally
displayed overhead. Nurses no longer wear the white hose and
red-cross caps of cartoons and pornography, but scrubs printed
with patterns so relentlessly cheerful—hearts, teddy bears, suns
and flowers and peace signs—they seem symptomatic of some
Pollyannaish denial. The smell of hospitals is like small talk at
a funeral—you know its function is to cover up something else.
There's a grim camaraderie in the halls and elevators. You don't
have to ask anybody how they're doing. The fact that they're there
at all means the answer is: Could be better. I notice that no one
who works in a hospital, whose responsibilities are matters of life
and death, ever seems hurried or frantic, in contrast to interns
at magazines I've known who weren't even allowed to leave for
lunch lest they be urgently needed.

Time moves differently in hospitals—both slower and faster.
The minutes stand still, but the hours evaporate. The day is long
and structureless, measured only by the taking of vital signs, the
changing of IV bags, medication schedules, occasional tests, meal-
times, trips to the bathroom, walks in the corridor. Once a day an
actual doctor appears for about four minutes, and what she says
during this time can either leave you and your family in terrified
confusion or so reassured and grateful that you want to write her
a thank-you note she'll have framed. You cadge six-ounce cans of
ginger ale from the nurses' station. You no longer need to look at
the menu in the diner across the street. You substitute meat loaf for
bacon with your eggs. Why not? Breakfast and lunch are diurnal

conventions that no longer apply to you. Sometimes you run errands back home for a cell phone or extra clothes. Eventually you look at your watch and realize visiting hours are almost over, and feel relieved, and then guilty.

My mother had been moved out of the ICU into a "step-down" unit by the time I arrived. Mom, who'd taught nursing for twenty years, was, like most medical professionals, a difficult patient—fretting about potential complications, second-guessing her doctors, tying to micromanage her treatment. My sister could gauge her condition from reading signs like her heart rate, temperature, and white cell count, but I had to gauge it from trying to read my sister. When, on the second day, Mom's fever broke, and everybody started using the phrase "turned the corner," I understood that she was going to live. After another day or two my sister went back to her job and family in Boston, while I would stay on with Mom for a few weeks while she recuperated. It was one of those occasions when you have to forget about the month you had planned out in your datebook and accept that what you're going to be doing instead is mostly nothing.

Hospital stays are one of the few times in adulthood when we have an excuse to drop all the busywork that normally preoccupies us and go to be with the people we love. You simply spend time with them, without any social occasion for it—a wedding or anniversary, dinner or the theater. You just sit there in the same room, making small talk or reading, offering the dumb comfort of your presence. You are literally There for them. When you're a kid, this is one of the dullest, most dehumanizing things you're forced to do—being dressed up in a navy blazer or a sweater vest and dragged to family reunions to be fawned over like a photo in an album, your physical presence all that's required of you. But if you manage to make it to some semblance of adulthood, just showing up turns out to be one of the kindest, most selfless things you can do for someone. And it isn't only selfless. At the beginning of my stay, my friend Lauren told me over the phone, "I know this seems like a drag, but someday, I promise you, you will look back and be grateful that you had this time with your mother."

Since my childhood my mother's and my love for one another has been refracted through the medium of art. I think it was easier for her to infer what might be going on in my head by reading over my shoulder than by asking me. She kept an eye on the Warner Bros. cartoons I watched on Saturday mornings and found them almost as funny as I did. She was especially fond of that lothario Pepé Le Pew, admiring his dauntless confidence (one of the same qualities, come to think of it, that must have first attracted her to my father, who in college was also something of a dandy). We made a point of watching the annual airings of movies like *Blazing Saddles, Airplane!,* and the *Pink Panther* films together (Mom's favorite line from *Blazing Saddles* was "Hey, where's de white women at?!"). When I was fifteen, more inscrutable than ever, she noticed me cracking up over a copy of *Catcher in the Rye,* which she hadn't been under the impression was meant to be a funny book. She surreptitiously read it herself to gauge my emotional health and discovered, to her relief, that it was. After that, throughout my teen years, we traded book recommendations, like Nabokov's *Pale Fire,* a subtler comedy than *Return of the Pink Panther* but not entirely dissimilar; there are jokes about sodomy and halitosis in *Pale Fire,* and its fictitious annotator, Charles Kinbote, is no less clueless or deluded of his own greatness than Messrs. Clouseau and Le Pew.

Unfortunately all the books I'd packed with me for this trip were the sorts of enduringly unenjoyable classics you assign yourself out of literary guilt. My reasoning had been that a long hospital stay might have the same effect as grad school; deprived of any more entertaining alternatives, I would be driven into a state of such consciousness-altering boredom that Dostoyevsky would be fun. But half a chapter of *Moby-Dick* made Mom sleepy, and she ixnayed *Crime and Punishment* after the author's introduction.

"Isn't that about an old lady getting hit with an axe?" she asked. "It sounds kind of depressing."

Tristram Shandy turned out to be ideal sickroom reading. Reading Sterne's mock-pompous prose aloud, my voice found an ambling cadence, and, in a kind of benign possession, assumed what I imagined was Sterne's arch, deadpan tone. Gradually we acclimated to the pace of a world with less to do, when reading aloud from the latest installment might be an evening's entertainment. To call *Tristram Shandy* "slow" would be missing the point, like calling *The Master and Margarita* implausible or *Huck Finn* a little broad. *Tristram Shandy* isn't slow so much as static, occasionally retrograde. Laurence Sterne seems to take a perverse, almost sadistic pleasure in thwarting our need for narrative progress. His titular hero, whose history the novel ostensibly is, is not even born until well into Book (not chapter, *Book*) III. At one point his uncle Toby starts to tap ash from his pipe and, what with various digressions and flashbacks, doesn't finish tapping it out until eleven chapters later. The Story of the King of Bohemia and His Seven Castles has to be begun no fewer than five times, each time being interrupted by Toby's enthusiastic suggestions and refinements.[2] Come to think of it, Tristram's life begins with a false start—or, rather, doesn't, quite: the Shandys set off for London to give birth in civilized surroundings, per a prenuptial agreement, only to be told it was a false alarm, and head back home again.

Every time we came to one of these false starts, dead ends, or circuitous detours that brought us back where we'd started, my mother would give Sterne, via me, the same kind of look she used to give my father when he got to the dénouement of one of the long, increasingly improbable stories he was fond of telling—a kind of affectionate disgust, amused despite herself, understanding very well that her exasperation was itself the punch line. Sterne, like my dad, knew how to string an audience along; he constantly drops little hints of hot gossip to come, like the scandal of Aunt Dinah and the coachman, or the story of Uncle Toby's amours. When, in the very last volume of the book, we finally arrive at the long-promised wooing of the Widow Wadman, it commences with three chapters: one blank, one a transcription of the march "Lillebullero" (which Toby is wont to whistle in times of stress), and one that begins (if you'll permit me to quote at length):

```
    __*     *     *     *     *     *     *     *     *
*     *     *     *     *     *     *     *     *
*     *     *     *     *     *     *     *     *
      *     *     *     *     *     *     *     *
*     *     *     *     *     *     *     *     *
*     *     *.__
```

Eventually Mom and I came to regard Sterne's suspenseful teasers at the end of each volume, such as "The reader will be content to wait for a full explanation of these matters till the next year,—when a series of things will be laid open which he little expects,"[3] with a somewhat jaundiced eye. Interpolations like "But this by the bye" were so self-evidently redundant they could not be other than jokes. By this point we knew it was pretty much *all* by the bye.

"One has to surrender unconditionally to Sterne's caprices" is Nietzsche's advice, "—always in the expectation, however, that one will not regret doing so."[4] Once we'd accepted that nothing was ever going to happen in *Tristram Shandy,* our expectation that anything ought to have started to seem stodgy and humorless. It turned out to be very much in the tradition of the silly plotless films Mom and I had always enjoyed—or, rather, they turn out to have been in its. *Tristram Shandy* flouts its obligations as a novel in the same way that *Blazing Saddles* and *Airplane!* mock the whole idea of a movie. Sterne affects to lament his resolute lack of progress: "Is it not a shame to make two chapters of what passed in going down one pair of stairs?" he sighs after Walter Shandy and his brother Toby have in fact spent a whole chapter getting down one flight.

"For we are got no farther yet than to the first landing, and there are fifteen more steps down to the bottom and for aught I know, there may be as many chapters as steps."[5] In the next chapter, Walter takes a single step down the next staircase, which almost makes you want to cheer, but he hesitates there and starts another conversation—and then, agonizingly, he actually *backtracks*, withdrawing his foot from the stair and walking all the way back across the landing to lean against the wall. You can't help but laugh at this, even if it's with that grudging admiration that says: *Ahh, you bastard.* But the conversation that Walter and Toby have on the landing, about women and pregnancy, is one of my favorites in the book. It's as if Sterne were saying, *Now wasn't that worth waiting for? And you were in such a rush.* He never does get them off the staircase; in the end, he leaves it up to the reader and even inquires, all innocent curiosity, how you managed to do it.

A physical therapist showed me how to help my mother climb stairs—a slow, laborious, two-feet-per-step procedure, painstaking as rock climbing. I had to remain a step below her, holding her elbow, ready to catch her in case she fell. Mom had recovered sufficiently to be moved to a hospital with a physical therapy program, where she would regain enough mobility to live independently again. She described herself as "something of a star" in physical therapy. "Apparently they don't see a whole lot of people who're in as good shape as I am," she said. The therapist also demonstrated how to help Mom get in and out of cars, a meticulous swiveling operation that kept her center of gravity directly over her feet. She showed us strategies for getting things out of the fridge or down off shelves, and suggested rearrangements of furniture for maximum convenience and economy of motion. We were like astronauts training for zero-g underwater: the simplest tasks had to be thought out, planned, and orchestrated, performed in slow motion and taken (literally) step by step.

I'm an impatient person. I take stairs two at a time; I can't stand getting trapped behind a phalanx of schoolkids or tourists on the sidewalk; a computer taking seven seconds to perform some operation is maddening to me. I hate all the boring in-between parts of life. Seeing my mother barely able to rise from a sitting to a standing position unaided, or shuffling slowly from the bed to the bathroom, made me furious for reasons I could not understand. Watching her tug feebly at some plastic packaging, I wanted to rip it open for her; waiting as she groped for a word, I had to restrain myself from yelling it. Since middle age Mom's taken longer and longer to retrieve proper nouns—the first words we learn and, she advises me, the first to go—but now the waits were getting excruciating. She and I had a history of conversations in which she would switch topics without any sort of signaling segue, and we would continue talking, unbeknownst to us, about two different things, the dialogue becoming increasingly Ionescan until we'd stop and stare at each other in bafflement and have to backtrack to the point where we'd diverged. The most famous of these had conflated the repair of my car with the completion of the Chief Crazy Horse Memorial in South Dakota, yielding what seemed to both of us like really unreasonable time and cost estimates. (It was not unlike the misunderstanding occasioned by Uncle Toby's shocking offer to show Mrs. Wadman "the very place" where he received his war wound, which is resolved only when he produces a map.) But when we had another of these exchanges in the hospital, I wasn't so amused. I probably don't have to tell you that getting mad at your own mother for being old and sick does not make you feel like a model son or exemplary human being. Getting irritated at my own irritability did not improve matters. It made me only a little more forgiving of myself to understand that my anger was mostly fear.

I wonder whether this same fear isn't beneath our twenty-first-century intolerance for waits and downtime and silence. It's as if, if we all had to stand still and shut up and turn off our machines for one minute, we'd hear the time passing and just start screaming. So instead we keep ourselves perpetually stunned with stimuli, thereby missing out on the very thing we're so scared of losing. Sterne's stairway is a perfect metaphor for all those tedious interstitial moments we can't wait to get through that make up most of our lives; we don't even think of stairways as places in themselves, only as a means to get somewhere else. I remember children's stories about kids who were granted the power to effectively fast-forward their lives, skipping all the homework and chores to get right to the good parts—driver's license, girlfriend, being a grown-up. Inevitably, they ripped through their whole lives in no time and found themselves suddenly old, looking back on a blank, elided lifetime without even memories to show for it. We're all so eager, both in life and in art, to get past this bullshit to the next Good Part up ahead. Believe it or not, Sterne's telling us, this bullshit *is* the good part. *I know this seems like a drag, but I promise you, someday you will be grateful you had this time with your mother.* All those digressions *were* the story. With his tortuous nonplot he's trying to tease us out of our insatiable impatience for narrative, our silly urgency to know What Next. It occurs to me now that the line Harold was so fond of quoting, Mrs. Shandy's question to her husband that interrupts his ejaculation, dooming the homunculus Tristram to a life of misfortune—"Pray, my Dear, have you not forgot to wind up the clock?"—is an intrusion of time and obligation into what should've been pure, unself-conscious pleasure in the moment. In effect, Sterne's saying, *Relax. What's your hurry? We'll get there soon enough—all too soon, in fact. And once we arrive, the fun will be over. So why not enjoy the company?* He knows that all journeys, and all stories, have the same ending, at a place nobody wants to go.

One reason my mother was so slow to recover her mobility was that she suffers from Parkinson's disease. Its onset was late and her symptoms were still minor—the most noticeable one was a tremor in her left hand if she missed her medication—plus Mom's official policy is 100 percent positivity in regard to all things, so around her kids, at least, she tended to minimize her diagnosis, saying she didn't want us worrying about her. All of which makes it easy to ignore the fact that the condition is progressive and incurable. During her sepsis she had also suffered what physicians call "an insult to the brain"—in this case a shortage of oxygen—so I could no longer be sure what was just Mom and what might be cognitive deficits. *Insult*—it's an apt description for all the indignities of age and infirmity. All the equipment she was being taught to use— walkers and rails and plastic shower stools—seemed humiliating and infantile to me, like being confined to cribs and high chairs all over again at the other end of life. Here I was reading aloud to the woman who used to read *The Snowy Day* and Fantastic Four comics to me.

Tristram Shandy is such a lighthearted book that it's easy to forget it was written by a man who'd known he was terminally ill since his twenties. From time to time he gripes in asides about his "vile cough," but he never names the dreaded disease, tuberculosis. His professed philosophy of "Shandyism" is a defiant frivolity that declines to take the world as seriously as it tries to insist upon. In the same way that he discreetly elides the catastrophe of Uncle To-by's courtship with censorious asterisks and alludes to some heart-break with one "Jenny" through dark apophasis, he always averts his eye from death, as when he declines to describe a soldier's last moments: "... shall I go on?—No."[6] His one-step-forward-eleven-steps-back structure is a stalling tactic; all that defiant idling is a little passive-aggressive fun at Death's expense. Look at the dia-grams he's drawn of his previous chapters' chronologies, like paro-dies of the Aristotelian dramaturgical ramp: leapfrogs, corkscrews, and French curls, jagged flashbacks, drooping detours, and long, meandering ox-bows, the author dragging his feet in his reluctance to arrive at tedious, predictable Point B. Four volumes into his life story he pauses to take stock of his progress and realizes that he's gotten only as far as Day One of his life, and that it's taken him a year to write, so that another 365 days to write about have piled up in the meantime. "It must follow, an' please your worships, that the more I write, the more I shall have to write—and consequently the more your worships will have to read."[7] This idea that as long as he lives he'll have even more to write has an illogical corollary: as long as he keeps writing, he won't die.[8] With all his evasions and deferments, by constantly adding on more stairs and days, Sterne's trying to turn time's arrow into Zeno's.[9]

At a certain age our parents offhandedly start telling us things we've never heard before, about themselves and their families, their upbringing and history. They're turning their lives into stories, trying to make sense of them in retrospect and pass them on while there's still time. You begin, embarrassingly belatedly, to see them as people with lives long preceding your own. A number of the old family stories Mom told me in the hospital suggested a weird streak of histrionic aggression toward fruit: a great-grandfather chopping down his whole orchard after failing to sell any apples at market, Uncle Harvey defiantly eating an entire bag of oranges at the Canada/U.S. border rather than allow them to be confiscated. She told me that her own mother had subscribed to a then-prevalent philosophy of childrearing consisting of two rules: 1) treat all your children equally and 2) raise the first one right so she can help you raise the rest of them. It seemed never to occur to her that these two rules were in any conflict. She appointed her oldest daughter, Helga, as her lieutenant and charged her with the responsibility of overseeing the three younger siblings, who, needless to say, rebelled, calling Helga "the Sarge," which made the Sarge cry. When Helga was born, my grandmother said she wouldn't take a million dollars for this baby, and wouldn't give a nickel for any other. "And then I had three nickel babies," she'd laugh. She used to call my mother a pill. "Lydia is a pill," she would tell people, as if explaining a lisp or a lazy eye. Mom told me that when she met my father, a sharp-dressed kid who used idiosyncratic slang that may well have been of his own invention, like *Okey-dinah* and *Eat the wall,* "he was the first person who made me feel like I was something." She even told me, to my surprise, what his last words to her had been: * * * * * * * * * *.

This, I think, is what Sterne is doing in *Tristram Shandy.* Much as Mom and I liked Sterne's voice and wit and his high unseriousness, what we remember best about *Tristram Shandy* are its characters. Sterne makes affectionate fun of the harmless forms of madness that afflict men in middle age, after their biological duty has been discharged—what he calls their "hobby-horses." Walter Shandy has crackpot theories about the effects of Christian names, physiognomy, and the pineal gland on a child's character and fate, and compiles a comprehensive guide to the care and instruction of his son—a "*Trista-paedia.*" Uncle Toby is a man monomaniacally obsessed with the subject of military science—you have to avoid any careless allusion to it lest he start holding forth on ramparts and bastions, half-moons and ravelins, deploying maps and diagrams and using jackboots as mortars and threatening to lead you on a tour of his backyard battlefield—who literally would not harm a fly.* Remember that Tristram, our ostensible narrator, is writing as a grown man, and his father was already in his fifties when he was born, so it's likely that Walter Shandy and all the other characters he recalls so fondly—Uncle Toby, Trim, Dr. Slop and Obadiah—are gone. His portraits are drawn not from life but from memory—or from stories, since so much of the book takes place before Tristram's birth. By rearranging the dreary chronology of real life, Sterne shows us the people he loves alive in their ridiculous prime, rescuing them from the oblivion of the black page.

---

*Cf. every eccentric family in comedic history: James Thurber's brother faking a fever dream and standing over his father's bed saying "Get up, Buck [not his father's name]. Your time has come," Jean Shepard's father being bizarrely elated when the family car has a blowout at the chance to demonstrate he can change a tire in under eight minutes, etc.

Mom and I were back home, walking down the brick walk from the car to the house at a rate that seemed likely to take us at least five minutes to arrive at the door. To make conversation on the way I asked Mom whatever had happened to the neighbors' dog. This dog had been our dog Maggie's nemesis. We would see it at the top of the hill across the front pasture, right on the horizon line, a big black dog sitting just on our side of the fence and barking in a blatant provocation. Maggie hated this dog. She would sit staring at it intently, ears pointy, her whole body poised to charge, as if waiting for the order. "Maggie," I'd say, "Go get it!" and—

off she would go like a bottle rocket across the lawn, over the stone wall and up the adjoining pasture to the top of the hill in seven seconds flat. And the other dog would flee, successfully repelled!

"It died," my mother said smugly. "I always knew that dog would die."

"What do you mean?" I said. "What did it do?" I was imagining some fatal canine hamartia like chasing cars or eating pesticides.

"It got old and died," she said, with satisfaction.

Mom never heard the end of *Tristram Shandy*. No, no, she didn't die, Mom's just fine, don't you worry. In fact, a year after her collapse, she claims she can feel new connections forming in

her brain: she's learning moviemaking software, writing heterodox statements of faith, discovering graphic novels. She even went
ziplining in Costa Rica, which no way in hell would I. She just
kept falling asleep during Slawkenbergius's Tale, a pretty labored
double entendre in which a man with an extremely long nose sets
all of Strasburg in an uproar, and we never recovered from the
longueur. I eventually finished the book, though I'm not sure if
Laurence Sterne did. Scholars disagree as to whether *Tristram
Shandy* was ever finished or only interrupted. When Death turns
up at Shandy's door in Volume VII, he reacts with the aplomb of
Bugs Bunny: he flees. Sterne ducked him for as long as he could,
but the old bore finally caught up with him when he was fifty-five.
If he hadn't come to the end of his story, he had, at least, reached
a good leaving-off point, which is probably the best any of us can
hope for. One of his own characters pronounces the story "the best
of its kind, I ever heard." What my father said on his deathbed, at
age fifty-six, was: "It's been great."

On my last day in Maryland I took a walk around the farm,
revisiting landmarks from the map of my childhood that I hadn't
seen in years: the Big Rock, the Brainfruit Tree, the ford where
deer and cattle and us kids always crossed the stream. Maggie went
along with me. I am not what's called "a dog person," but my love
for this particular dog is unsound. The first time I saw her I ex-
claimed, "Why, but this is not like a dog at all! It is more like an
otter, or a seal!" She was short-haired and sleek and wiggly, with a
pointy snout. I immediately picked her up and held her up in the
air above my head. She went limp in my arms and looked gamely
around at the world from her new perspective. Whenever I get
out of my car at the farm now and see her loping up to me sort of
sidewise (which is how she's run ever since Mom accidentally ran
over her head with a riding mower years ago) and wagging her
tail, I behave like someone on a very short supervised visit from an
institution. "Maaaaag-gie!" I yell. "Mags Marie! Maggie Maroo!

Maggle! Magwort! Maaaaaaaaaaags!" I get down and hold her nose in my hand and nuzzle her face and whap her vigorously on the sides. Ah—a solid thump! A solid dog.

Maggie followed me around the whole perimeter of the seventy-acre property, down hills and across streams and through the woods, like a boy's best friend. But Maggie is an old dog now, over fourteen, and the effort to keep up exhausted her. On the last steep hillside before home her feeble hind legs gave out on her, and she collapsed onto her haunches, panting helplessly up at me. She would live only a few months longer; someone ran over her a second time, and this time it took. I crouched down next to her and put my arms around her. "O Maggie," I told her, "you're the fastest dog in the world." I whispered it in her ear: *"The fastest dog in the world."*

Sister World

My half sister Sophie and I talk sometimes about how weirdly normal our relationship feels after having known each other only a year. She lives three blocks from me now, and we get together for dinner or drinks once every couple of weeks. We're like pals. But every once in a while I'll throw an extra tablespoon of capers into a sauce on a whim and she'll tell me, "My mother makes this same recipe, and she always adds extra capers, too," or I'll be distracted from our conversation by her eyes, the same blue as my own, and the strangeness of it all makes us shiver. She knows what certain fleeting half expressions on my face mean—she can, in a sense, read my mind. Not many of us see our siblings as particularly miraculous; they're more like randomly assigned roommates we had to live with for eighteen years. As Sophie once put it, most people don't think about their biological connection to their families in the same way that, after about age seven, they quit thinking about the sky—wondering why it's blue, why it turns red at sunset, how high it goes, what clouds are made of, how come they don't fall down. "But the sky is pretty cool," she insisted. I nodded soberly. "The sky is cool," I admitted.

I'd always thought of being adopted as being about as interesting and significant a fact about myself as being left-handed or having family in Canada. What seems freakish and fascinating to me is something so commonplace most people take it for granted: being related. As an outsider and a newcomer to this phenomenon—what people call kinship, or blood—I may have a privileged perspective on it, like Tocqueville visiting America. What's so familiar to you it's invisible still seems outlandish to me. For most people the bonds of blood and history are inextricable, but I experienced them in isolation from one other, just as my transgendered friend Jenny has had the rare vantage of living as both a man and a woman. Meeting biological relatives for the first time in midlife, I felt like one of those people, blind from birth, whose vision is surgically restored, and must blunder about in an unintelligible new world, learning, through trial and error, how to see. You can't understand the word *blue* until you see the sky for the first time.

I had a family growing up, like you probably did. We were even a happy one, as families go. My parents were smart and kind and funny and encouraged all my weird interests and never kept me from reading anything I wanted to. My sister Laurie and I sometimes played elaborate imaginary games together, and sometimes threatened to kill each other. We watched *Sesame Street* and *The Brady Bunch* and *M*A*S*H*. We had dogs and cats, a carousel slide projector and Super 8 home movies, big American Christmas mornings. We went to church and to Disney World. People who didn't know that my sister and I were adopted told us we looked just like our parents. But I didn't meet anyone I was related to until I was in my forties.

I'd always known I was adopted; it was part of the answer to the Where-did-I-come-from question. The parental talking point was that I had been *chosen* by people who loved and wanted me, unlike all those other kids who'd just come down the chute by chance. I never felt like I'd been abandoned, or suffered any loss or trauma, or yearned to be reunited with my original parents, imagining that finding them would be some sort of answer to the question of Me. I felt as if I'd won some sort of lottery when I was adopted; a lot of my friends and cousins envied me my parents, who seemed so open-minded and supportive compared to their own. I always imagined that people for whom being adopted was a major issue must have had deficient or abusive upbringings, been damaged or deprived in some way. Having common genes seemed to me almost as arbitrary as sharing a home state or zodiac sign, and anyone who fixated on such a flimsy bond must've been groping for any connection at all.

Years ago one of my adopted friends and I agreed over beers that we secretly thought being adopted made us cooler than other people, more American—less encumbered by all the dreary baggage of heritage and history, freer to invent ourselves, like young Jimmy Gatz or Bruce Wayne. This has since proven to be not entirely true. You learn that your personality has a certain shape, with definite, inflexible bounds—bounds you find out about because you keep bonking into them headfirst when you try to change. (An acquaintance who used to grate on me won me over when I overheard her sigh, "D'ya ever wish you could just . . . trade in your whole personality for a new one?") We are not infinitely malleable. Like it or not, you are a certain kind of person. Life is, in this respect, like that game in which you're assigned an identity scrawled on a piece of paper that everyone else can see but you can't, and you have to try to deduce from other people's hints and snickers who you are. It doesn't matter if you want to be Pierre Bonnard or Vasco da Gama if what's written on your card is *Barney Rubble*. Eventually you give up and ask, *Okay: so who am I?*

Around the time I turned forty, the age at which physicians recommend you start lying awake worrying about your health, I decided I'd be well advised to request whatever medical history I could get from the adoption agency. This, at least, was my ostensible reason for contacting them, although practicality and self-maintenance

are qualities so unlike me that there must have been other, less conscious motives at work. Forty is also an age when our life spans start
to look alarmingly finite, and it had occurred to me that my biological mother would be sixty-one by now, which wasn't old but wasn't
young, either. I didn't even know for certain that she was still alive.

I applied to the adoption agency for what's called "nonidentify-
ing information" about my biological mother—medical and family
history, everything but names and places. Unexpectedly, the agency
sent me an entire file of information garnered from my mother's in-
take interview, about not only herself and her family but the circumstances of my birth and adoption—the whole nativity story of me.
It was certainly more than most people ever get to hear about their
own conceptions. I'd hesitated before opening this file, a little reluc-
tant to surrender the privilege of ignorance. After I read it, however
unique or interesting my story might prove to be, it would be forever
fixed as one thing and not another; the mystery of myself would be
solved, limitless possibility replaced with plain old facts.

It was, of course, an ordinary human story, messy and painful
and typical of millions that took place around that time. This is not
wholly my own story to tell, so I'll suffice it to say that my existence
turns out to have been contingent on a number of people behaving
with extraordinary decency in difficult circumstances. It was also,
I feel obliged to mention, contingent on the fact that I was born six
years before *Roe v. Wade.* This hasn't changed my position on abor-
tion, but it does make me feel like the beneficiary of some unfair
historical loophole, like having missed out on the draft. It all made
my life seem even more undeserved than it already did, as though
the world were a private party I'd gotten to crash.

One of the factoids that caught my attention, among all the
dates and ages and figures in that family history, was that my ma-
ternal grandfather had been 5 foot 10 inches and 150 pounds, with
brown hair and blue eyes—my height, weight, and coloration exactly. This is hardly a bizarre coincidence, but to me it seemed al-

most uncanny, like a ghost story in which you find an image of yourself in a photo taken before you were born. The most basic facts about me were not wholly my own; it was as if I no longer belonged exclusively to myself. *Well,* you may well point out, *duh.* Like everyone else in the world, I come from someone else. *Omni cellula e cellula,* dude. Of course it's absurd to imagine that any of us appeared ex nihilo, but I hadn't even been aware that I'd harbored this delusion until I was disabused of it.

I put all this information in a file folder on my desk, where it sat, getting shuffled slowly to the bottom of the pile and then pulled out and put back on top, for the next four years. If I wanted to initiate contact with my biological mother, all I had to do was fill out a rather patronizing touchy-feely questionnaire required by the state ("Have you considered what your reaction might be if your birth parent does not consent to contact you at this time? If not, give it some thought now") and write her an introductory letter, which the agency would forward if they could locate her. I wasn't conscious of avoiding this next step; it just seemed like I kept not getting around to it, the same way I keep not getting around to planning for retirement. And composing a letter to the mother you've never met is the kind of assignment that could keep any writer procrastinating and rewriting for years. I am not privy to what was going on in my mind during this time, but obviously I was somehow readying myself, filling out my own internal questionnaire.

The decisive factor may have been that I found myself in a potentially narrow window in my life during which I felt I could plausibly present myself as having turned out okay. So one afternoon when I was visiting home, on what seemed like impulse I drove into Baltimore and dropped the form and my letter off at the adoption agency—a big Gothic cottage with steep gables and gingerbread molding, like a house from a fairy tale. I then tried to forget about them, telling myself that I might not hear anything back for months, or years, if ever. I was bracing myself against this possibility because never hearing anything back from women happens to be my very least favorite thing in life, and this was, after all, the very first woman I'd never heard from again.

I'd failed to prepare myself for the opposite possibility, which was that I would hear back from her almost immediately. In less than two weeks I got a call from the agency letting me know they'd received a reply from my birth mother, which they would forward to me the next day. (She told me later she would've responded even sooner, but she'd been away on vacation when my letter arrived.) It was like one of those scenes in a movie where someone takes a running start to bust down a door, only to have someone open it cordially from the other side.

I didn't open her reply right away. I was stricken with a kind of stage fright. I actually brushed my teeth. It felt like a formal occasion. I emailed a friend of mine the message: "Eeeeeeeeeeeeeeeeeeeeeeeee." Sitting on the desk in front of me was a handwritten letter from my biological mother, a person who had always seemed less vividly real to me than Robin Hood.

Her name was Rachel. Last name Dillon, née Campbell. She lived not much more than an hour from where I'd grown up. Her letter reciprocated the tone of my own—cautious and deferential, eager to avoid any intrusion or demands. She reassured me that it was a relief to hear from me, and to know that I'd been raised by people who loved me. After having me she hadn't had children for twenty years—apparently we'd both walked away from the experience of childbirth with unhappy associations—but then in her forties she'd divorced, remarried, and had two daughters. *I've lived a happy life that often felt like a second chance,* she wrote. *It has added to that happiness to hear from you.* She'd also enclosed some photos: there was one of herself as a little girl with her family, a kid who's doted on and knows it, face squinched up in a simper, fingers at her dimples; one as a young woman a few years after she'd had me, a thin blonde in big seventies sunglasses whom my friend Jenny described as "you, in drag"; and a recent one of her husband and herself on the street, looking like a kindly couple of college professors. Lastly, there was a photo of her two daughters, Sophie, age twenty-three, and Amy, twenty-one—my half sisters.

I had asked her in my letter whether I had any half siblings as much out of courtesy as any genuine curiosity. What I'd really wanted to ask was too big to articulate, and this was one of the few specific questions I could think of. But now, looking at this photograph of two young women I did not know, something very strange happened in my head. They were standing on the back steps of a wooden house, with a green lawn and woods in the background. It could've been a suburban home or a summer cottage. They were smiling—one radiantly, the other more shyly—their arms around each other's shoulders. The older one had brown hair, like mine; the younger was blond. They looked happy, well cared for, and fond of one another. "No way are those girls related to you," my friend Kevin wrote me after seeing the photo. "They are beautiful and, well, just look at you." I had to concur. It was hard to believe they could have anything to do with me. It took my friends to point out to me that Amy, the younger one, had the same nose I did. I had to compare photos of the two of us before I could see the similarity, but once I did, I couldn't stop looking at it. I kept staring at that picture of these two girls I did not know, trying to understand what they were.

Sophie and Amy, meanwhile, who had never been told that their mother had had a previous child, intuited that something was up. (All this I learned from them later, in debriefing over cocktails.) Their mother had been drifting around the house in an absent, dreamy way, dropping cryptic remarks about the past, like some haunted Gothic heroine. At the same time, she seemed happier than they'd ever seen her—lighter, younger. Sophie almost wondered whether she could be having an affair. Amy caught her compiling what looked like a family medical history on her laptop, and asked her what it was for. Her mother yelped, "I don't have to tell you everything!" and snapped the laptop shut. In a deductive coup worthy of Nancy Drew, Amy called up her sister, who was visiting New York for the weekend and was at that moment in the Metropolitan Museum of Art, and said: "So I think we might have a secret half sibling." Sophie sat down on a bench.

When friends asked me how I felt before going to meet my biological mother for the first time, my honest answer was: *I have no idea.* The emotions involved were too vast for me to detect, like our solar system's quarter-billion-year revolution around the galactic center. I went into that meeting with the same here-goes fatalism with which I embark on first dates: at this point in my life I figure it's no use trying to cover up who I am—I just show up and say *This is me* and hope they don't hate me. Panicking at the last minute and in need of props, I took along some visual aids—old baby photos and childhood drawings, in case she wanted to know what she'd missed. At the last minute the disquieting thought occurred to me that although as far as I was concerned this was our first meeting, she would remember me. I wondered whether I would recognize her smell.

The first time Rachel saw me it gave her an ache she described as like homesickness, because she'd thought the last member of her father's side of the family, the devilish-eyed Campbell clan, had died off, but now she saw one of them, still alive. Innocuous expressions I wasn't even conscious of making—an equivocal shrug of the eyebrows, mouth tugged to one side in chagrin—gave her chills of recognition. I know that I look like Rachel because friends I haven't introduced her to yet can easily pick her out of a crowd, but the resemblance must be so obvious that it's invisible to me, like the off-putting strangeness of your own recorded voice.

There were a number of similarities between us, some of them all the more unsettling because they seemed so trivial. We're both atheists; apparently her father had been a nonbeliever in the fifties, and Rachel had actually hoped to make it a condition of my adoption that I not be given to religious parents. (I had to break it to her that I'd been raised by Mennonites, but reassured her I'd turned out godless anyway.) We were both passionately opinionated leftists of the school that holds that political change is best effected through strident ranting over drinks. It emerged that we'd been celebrating in adjacent bars on the National Mall in Washington on Inauguration Day in 2009. We had the same favorite scotch—Lagavulin, a rarefied taste, so rich and peaty that a whiff of it singes your eyelids. When I mentioned that I baked pies, Rachel's face went suddenly still and wary, like a deer hearing a rustle in the underbrush. "Who taught you to make pies?" she asked. "No one," I shrugged. "I just started making them." "*I* make pies," she told me, almost accusingly. "My father made pies—he was *known* for his pies. *His* mother made pies." It was as if a pie gene had switched on in my thirties. Somehow this was even stranger to me than the possibility that my deepest beliefs and political convictions were predetermined. It only makes sense that something like palate would be heritable, but it was still disquieting to learn that what felt like a choice was encoded, as if I were a character in a Philip K. Dick story who learns that what he thought were his memories have been programmed.

A week after meeting Rachel for the first time, I had dinner with the entire family: Rachel, her husband, Simon, and their daughters, Sophie and Amy. They knew about me by now; Rachel had finally sat them down and said, *Listen: there's something I haven't told you.* I was even more circumspect in approaching Sophie and Amy than I'd been with their mother, who had, at least, known about me all along. I was a little embarrassed by my unexpected existence. I could only imagine how profoundly weirded out I would've been to learn, in my twenties, that I had a half sibling twenty years older than me. Meeting me must have been, for them, like suddenly inheriting a llama ranch. On the hand: Llamas! Hey! Neat. On the other: So, uh, what exactly does one do with a llama, anyway?

Rachel and Simon did most of the talking at dinner, bickering in a familiar pro forma way about politics, while Sophie and Amy and I mostly stole looks at each other across the table. They were lovely young women, luminous with youth, the awkwardness of adolescence still clinging to them. Sophie still sometimes assumed the gawky, unself-conscious poses of a girl on a bed full of stuffed animals; when I'd ask Amy a question she'd duck her head and answer in a flustered dismissive rush that forced you to crane forward to hear. Sophie was the more forthcoming one; I could tell already that Amy tended to go quiet around her older sister. But I also thought I caught glimmers of an affinity between us, the way you'll see someone at a party and know right away you're going to like them. I noticed our eyes were all the same blue.

After dinner, Sophie and Amy and I went out for a drink, just us kids. The three of us sat on plush lounge chairs having martinis, all being excessively courteous and self-conscious and frantically curious about each other. We were trying to catch up on twenty years in one night; it was hard to bear in mind, or believe, that we were going to know each other for the rest of our lives. We exchanged birthdays and middle names. Sophie said that, in retrospect, knowing about me made so much sense of so many things about their—our—mother. We all stared at each other and said *whoah,* spooked by the words "*our* mother." We were improvising the rules of our relationship as we went along, abruptly overconfiding, catching ourselves and feeling embarrassed, then figuring *aah, screw it, we're related* and blundering ahead. "Half-sibling protocol," we called it. We invented our own self-congratulatory familial toast. They confessed that they'd always fantasized, in a childish, daydreamy way, about having an older brother. "We're just so happy you exist," said Sophie.

Years ago when my friend Carol, who was also adopted, had her first child, she called me and said, "I'm telling you, Tim—you gotta have kids. It's incredible." I'm afraid I may actually have laughed at her. It seemed so presumptuous, like strangers showing up on your doorstep expecting you to switch religions before they leave. I charitably attributed her advice to hormonal delirium and forgot about it until the day, years later, when I met my own biological family. It was only then that I understood what Carol had been trying to tell me: what it was like to know someone you were related to for the first time in your life.

I am a terrible man who routinely deletes the baby pictures people send me without a glance. (Sorry, they're babies—they all look the same.) I'd heard stories about new fathers being zapped with overwhelming love for their newborns, all rational misgivings instantly vaporized, and had regarded these reports the way I did the testimonials of the born again, as subjectively real and powerful experiences that were evidently inaccessible to me, like schizophrenia. But now, embarrassingly, I was acting like a new father myself: mentioning my new sisters on tenuous pretexts, boring people with little stories about them, foisting their photos on polite acquaintances. I emailed a picture of my sisters and myself to friends with, as its only caption, an exclamatory string of little heart emoticons. My friend Annie replied: "Who *are* you?" I sounded exactly as deluded as parents do gushing about their exceptional children: they were so intelligent and preternaturally self-aware, so far ahead of anywhere I was when I was their age, such lovely, warm, openhearted young women. Listening indulgently, my friends just smiled, genuinely happy for me but not without a certain toldja-so amusement. I had never been so blindsided by affection.

It certainly helped that Sophie and Amy were exactly the kinds of people I would've hoped they'd be if I'd tried to imagine them. Sophie had majored in psychology—and she was intimidatingly astute at reading people—but she also loved to write. Her favorite novel, *Infinite Jest,* was also one of mine. Amy was a serious and insightful reader, too, and also doodled compulsively. Her

mother told me that she'd been doodling at a party when someone had commented that she sure liked to draw, and she'd said
casually: "Yeah, my brother's a cartoonist." (She had known about
me, at that point, for about three weeks.) They were very much
their own people, and yet I felt as if we were all the same *type* of
person: smarter than was good for us, prone to gloomy introspection, moody and oversensitive. We nurture hurts, flagellate ourselves over our failings, glumly anticipate worst-case scenarios.
We brood. (None of us can smoke marijuana—Amy describes it
as "like three hours of bad therapy.") When Sophie confided in
me the unprecedented and stressful dilemma of being in a stable
relationship with someone she really loved, I almost laughed with
sympathetic recognition. Yes, Sophie: happiness is indeed *a terrible
problem.* When Amy, remorseful over some pretty typical youthful screwup—typical of her and me, at least—wrote me miserably:
"Alcohol, insecurity, poor judgment, and me have done me in," I
suggested we have this motto translated into Latin for our family
crest. I was sorry that so many of the traits I shared with my sisters
were such unpleasant ones to have, but I loved sharing them. Not
that it helps, of course; in the end, you're still stuck with the problem of You. But it's a relief to know that I'm not the only one.

Maybe I would've seen such seemingly profound similarities
in anyone I'd been told I was related to, the way everyone sees
themselves described with uncanny accuracy in generic horoscopes
("You are prone to gloomy introspection, moody and oversensitive . . ."). What if the adoption agency were to contact me and
say, *Oops, so sorry, very embarrassing, ha ha, but seems there was a
big mistake—that's not your family after all.* Would my affection for
them evaporate like our reverence for a Rembrandt when it turns
out to be an imitation? What if, instead of two smart, articulate,
funny half sisters who love New York and novels and bars, I'd had
two hulking monobrowed half *brothers* who'd wanted to take me
to a fucking lacrosse game? It's hard to believe I would've been as

smitten with those hypothetical lunkheads as I was with Sophie and Amy. Plenty of people have biological siblings with whom they have nothing in common—brothers who listen to Rush Limbaugh, sisters who think shopping is fun—and they still have to spend Thanksgiving with them. It's possible I just lucked out.

I felt like I had to dissemble my demented affection around my half sisters, lest they get the accurate impression that I was wildly overinvested in them way too soon. It was like being on a second date with someone you've already made up your mind you're going to marry. There is no imposition so presumptuous as other people's love, and it made me wince to imagine how it would seem to a young woman to have some forty-year-old guy suddenly show up out of nowhere all, like, *enamored* of you. But does it even make sense to talk about being "overinvested" in someone who shares half your genes? A friend of mine told me that the first time she saw her infant niece she knew instantly that she would donate a kidney to this person if she were ever to need one. Nobody loves newborns for who they are; they aren't anyone yet. ("You see how it is godlike to love the *being* of someone," the narrator tells his son in Marilynne Robinson's *Gilead*. "Your *existence* is a delight to us."[1]) What my friends were trying to tell me by sending me all those baby pictures wasn't the kind of information that's conveyed in a portrait; they were less like telegrams than fireworks.

"Do you think it'd be easier if we had kids?" my friend Annie asked me once. By "it" she was referring to life, which we were both finding had begun, only halfway through, to drag. Annie's mother had recently died, and mine was ill; Annie was brooding over an incipient wattle, while I'd been getting more root canals than I normally like. Studies have confirmed what's pretty obvious—having children makes people even unhappier. But what people want, above all else, is not to be happy; they want to devote themselves to something, to give themselves away. Some parents had told me that you couldn't understand what it meant to truly love someone until you'd had a child, which had always seemed to me like not a very impressive advertisement for human altruism—most people only ever experienced selfless love toward people who were genetic extensions of themselves? But now here it was, a force as matter-of-fact and implacable as the gravity of the planet, the deceptively gentle pull of six thousand sextillion tons.

Sophie and Amy were not my daughters, nor did I feel particularly paternal toward them—in fact, between their precocity and my own retardation I felt about five years older than they were—but for the first time I thought I had some inkling of why people had children. It made the next forty years seem worth hanging around for to have these two young women in my life, in whom I had some biological investment, whom I would get to see become adults. It was cheering to see some growth and development instead of constant, incremental decline. Like anyone who's lived long enough, I'd lost people—to addiction, mental illness, death and defriending, the irrefutable facts of peak oil, or just the attrition of time and distance—so it felt like a minor coup in the losing war against entropy, a temporary hedge against death, to get someone unexpectedly back. And it was exhilarating to discover within myself, at this late date, such a bottomless capacity for affection—an affection free, for once, from the complications of desire. It was like opening a window to let in the first fresh breeze of April after a long winter shut in with the stale smell of yourself.

Plus I took advantage of Sophie in a moment of uncritical gratitude and got her to agree to look after me in my old age. I'd just helped her to find her first postcollegiate job after a miserable interval of being unemployed and living at home, a well-paying position with full benefits that would allow her to move to New York City, her childhood dream. We were celebrating over a dinner she described as the best Chinese food she'd ever had. Still dazed, she said: "I just don't know how I'll ever be able to repay you for this."

"Take care of me when I'm old!" I said between bites of tongue-numbing Chong Qing chicken.

"Done!" she said. We shook on it. Now that I've put it in print she cannot renege.

I reassured her, in all seriousness, that she didn't need to worry about paying me back; it just didn't work like that. And, to my surprise, I meant it. Helping my new sisters was a pleasure in itself. To me these girls were like lost princesses of Mars who'd crash-landed behind my barn—I wanted to bring them offerings of our humble earth delicacies, sno-cones and dandelions and jars full of fireflies. I wanted to give them hypocritical advice, forbid them to do anything I'd ever enjoyed, shield them from the kinds of people I'd spent decades cultivating friendships with. I found myself, while standing in the shower or doing dishes, scheming nice things to do for them, plotting to advance their interests in the world. I could see now why nepotism, which is so shamelessly unjust, is also so widely shrugged at. It's only natural. Biological altruism! Genes—apparently they really work.

Of course, I was not an astonishing novelty to Sophie and Amy; they already had each other. They were also absorbed in the drama of young adulthood—trying to find jobs that weren't demeaning, apartments that weren't depressing cells, and boyfriends who weren't dangerous imbeciles, to figure out what they were supposed to be and how love worked and what life was for, all while having highly demanding amounts of fun that made it hard to concentrate. So I didn't get to take it personally or feel slighted if they forgot to call me back or flaked out or canceled at the last minute, as young people are known to do. It was the first time in my life I'd had to be the grown-up, a role at which I was unpracticed. But this was also the first relationship I'd had in which the usual rules of reciprocity felt irrelevant. I was doomed to adore these girls even if they thought of me as an obligation or a bother or a bore.

I was fooling myself, as perhaps most parents do about their children, about not wanting anything from my sisters. The things I wanted were just too large and scary to name. What I wanted was to be allowed to feel as if I belonged with them. "But you do belong," Sophie told me once, as though it were only natural, and not even up to her. It seemed too easy, like getting to be in the same club as Thomas Jefferson, Herman Melville, Robert Goddard, and Miles Davis by dumb luck of having been born an American. Once, over beers, I was clumsily trying to tell Amy how grateful I was that she and her sister had been so accepting of me, when they could as easily have been indifferent or jealous or hostile. She said simply: "You're family." I felt whatever's the opposite of heartbroken.

But of course it wasn't that easy. Just hearing Amy refer to me as "my brother" or writing "us kids" feels almost illicit, for the same reason that saying "my husband" out loud sounds funny and false to newlyweds. You don't automatically get to be family because you share DNA, any more than you truly get married by signing a license or reciting vows or kissing in front of all your relatives. Rachel gave birth to me, but it would never occur to me to call her "Mom." And it doesn't particularly thrill me to call my adoptive sister Laurie "my sister" because she's as much my sister as my arm is my arm. Sophie and Amy had seemed to me, at first, like an unexpected bonus, pure and uncomplicated—family without baggage. Which is, of course, not family at all. Family is all about baggage—feuds and grudges and long-unspoken tensions, having fights and being forced to apologize, enduring each other's unendearing foibles for decades. They are, like it or not, the people who won't go away.

Like a lot of siblings, my own sister and I—by which I mean Laurie, the sister I grew up with, who's also adopted, to whom I'm not related—don't seem to have much in common. She's a doctor, married to another doctor, with two kids, living in a big suburban house outside of Boston. I'm an artist and bachelor who lives in a studio in New York City. When they visit New York they see Broadway musicals and eat at chain restaurants in Times Square;

when I visit them I skulk around their house unsure what to do with myself and stay up late channel-surfing. These days we mostly see each other for holidays and emergencies. When our mother was in the hospital for a month Laurie and I had to spend several days in the town where we grew up, driving back and forth between the hospital and our childhood home, both of us yanked out of our own lives, sleep-deprived and scared. In the car, passing a supermarket, I'd ask her, "Did I ever tell you about the time Dad left me at that Safeway?" or she'd point at a tree and say, "That's where I had my first car accident." (I gave her an older-brother look of bemusement and contempt: "Your first accident was in the *driveway?*") She remembers the same grade school teachers I do, the old house on Green Spring Avenue, the imaginary country under the stairs. She remembers Dad. We may not have much to talk about anymore, but our voices still sound the same.

At family get-togethers Laurie still likes to retell the stories of how I dotted red food coloring onto her Raggedy Ann doll's throat to simulate a vampire bite and would read her passages from Stephen King aloud, which allegedly traumatized her. When she starts in with this routine I always make a pained, weary face as if to say, *Please, why must you do this, I beg of you.* I worry that these stories do not reflect particularly well on me and can only imagine she tells them to publicly mortify me. I'm too obtuse to understand that—in addition to, yes, maybe taking a little vindictive pleasure in making me squirm—she's trying to talk about our shared past, and her love for me. I don't have to worry that I'm somehow going to blow it with Laurie—I've already blown it. She knows all about me. We've shared a bedroom. I walked her down the aisle. I'm her brother. I have granted this woman the legal power to remove me from a ventilator, even though there is still a small gray mark in the ball of her thumb where I once stabbed her with a pencil.

Like indifferent parents who become extravagant, doting grand-parents, I felt as if meeting my half sisters was a chance to atone for my derelictions and finally get being an older brother right. I was forgetting that it's the scars that mark us as siblings. Amy apparently had a history of borrowing her older sister's clothes without always explicitly asking first. Once she borrowed one of Sophie's dresses—a coveted dress that she had not only not been granted permission but specifically forbidden to borrow—and wore it to a party where, in a moment of forgetful exuberance, she leapt into a swimming pool without first removing it. This incident came to light when an incriminating photograph was posted on a popular social networking site showing Amy at said party in the now sopping and translucent dress. Inevitably, this damning evidence was brought to Sophie's attention. "I *knew* there was something different about that dress," she seethed. This grievance festered for most of a summer. A punitive policy of Not Speaking was instituted for an indeterminate period, and a moratorium placed on all sororal loans or sharing of any kind. It was a tense several weeks around the Dillon household. The night that Sophie had left home to move to New York, Amy and I came back from having a beer and found that she had left the dress on Amy's bed, with a piece of notebook paper placed atop it on which was drawn a magic-markered heart. Seeing that note, I felt a pang of fondness, but also, faintly, of envy. It was a gesture that spoke of the kind of affection that's annealed out of a thousand little hurts and reconciliations. I would never be family to Sophie and Amy in the way they were to each other; we had never hit each other or told on each other or made each other cry. And I would remain an outsider to that intimacy until I did the thing I was most afraid of—doing or saying the Wrong Thing, blowing it somehow, making them go away.

Which had to happen sooner or later. The biggest events in life often take longest to affect us, and it was several months after we'd met when Amy wrote me to confess that she was feeling uncomfortable about how much more often I spoke or wrote to her and Sophie than to their mother. The day I got this email I spilled hot coffee on my leg and almost broke my nose walking facefirst into a metal pole on some piece of playground equipment. I tried to reassure her, without sounding too defensive, that my relationship with their mother was not less important to me than ours; it was, on the contrary, far more complicated, fraught with old issues and history. Amy didn't respond. That's just how she was, Sophie assured me—she needed time to work things through for herself. The next time I saw her it would be as if nothing had happened. I ought to have understood this well, since withdrawal has long been my own preferred method of conflict management, but it didn't make it any easier to wait out the silence, which is, as I may have mentioned, my least favorite thing.

Months later (after Amy had, per Sophie's prediction, come back as nonchalantly as a cat does after it's freaked out and fled) Sophie and I had a half-sibling summit talk of our own. She told me that, although she genuinely liked me, some of the issues my appearance had raised were catching up to her, and seeing me was, frankly, sometimes hard for her. She'd had to accept that what she'd thought of as the most basic facts about her family were untrue, or at least incomplete—that there weren't only four of them, that she wasn't the oldest child anymore—and some part of her was recoiling, having none of it, shaking her head saying *No!* She also asked me the question I'd dreaded: "Why do you *like* us so much?" She wasn't exactly creeped out or bothered so much as she just didn't get it. "Not that we're not likeable and all," she said, "but you *really* seem to like us." I made the mouth-tugged-to-the-side-with-chagrin face. Apparently I am not a CIA-level dissembler. I'd also forgotten that Sophie can read my mind. All I could tell her was that I was as helpless over my affection for her as she was over her own conflicted feelings about me. I genuinely like her and her sister, too—they're extraordinary people I'm glad I have an excuse to know—but I also love them, for reasons that have less to do with who they are as individuals than with what they are to me—a love that's as overwhelming and mysterious to me as it must seem weird and unprovoked to them. I can't expect them to understand this, any more than I'll ever be able to appreciate how Rachel must have felt not knowing for forty years what had happened to her son—what kind of people had raised him, if he ever thought of her on Mother's Day, whether he'd been killed in Iraq or Afghanistan—or how it must have felt to find him again.

I deliberately plunged into this undertaking without too much reflection, the way I'd volunteer to go into space if the opportunity presented itself, reasoning that if I thought through all the ways in which it could go wrong I might never do it at all. I'm still only beginning to understand how naïve and oblivious I've been to the tangled realities of the situation, and how disruptive my presence in these people's lives has been. We are enmeshed now, and because we're all so touchy and high-strung, our relationships seem likely to involve dramatic emotional ins and outs for some time. Rachel and I are proceeding more steadily but also more slowly, as if in gradually closing spirals. We've made strawberry-rhubarb pie together, and she taught me to use the leftover dough to make a treat her daughters call "roly-polys." She's also introduced me to some of my extended relations—cousins, second cousins, cousins in-law. This, finally, is beginning to feel like what I think of as family: being introduced and explained to people you don't know, having to remember names and genealogical connections, being instantly dismissed by ten-year-olds as another boring grown-up. It's a little like having in-laws—another family full of birthdays not to forget, idiosyncratic customs and etiquette not to breach, and hidden dynamics to try not to run afoul of. The honeymoon phase is over; we're beginning the long process of disenchantment. But disenchantment also means being freed, unblinded. We have the rest of our lives to get to know each other as people—ordinary, disappointing, surprising, and impossible.

But I hope we won't forget how we looked to one another in

those first days of discovery, when we first learned we weren't alone. The summer we met, Amy and I took a half-sibling field trip together to see a show of astronomical photographs at the National Air and Space Museum. We saw Mercury silhouetted against the inferno of the sun, a pebble cast into a lake of fire, the deranged landscape of Miranda, a little world shattered and imperfectly rejoined, and Saturn's rings arcing across its limb, like fine hairs against the curve of a cheek. It emerged that Amy had never touched the moon rock before, so we stood in line with all the other earthlings and waited our turn to run our fingers over its glassy surface, smoothed to a warm polish by millions of fingers before ours. Later, over oysters and beer at Old Ebbitt Grill, we were considering a stuffed walrus head on the wall above us when a man at the bar next to Amy said, "I see you're admiring my ex-wife," and as Amy threw back her head in delight I caught a startling glimpse of my own laughter in hers. Seeing my own goofy expressions transposed into beauty in her face was like seeing those filigreed blue shadows fall over Saturn's lambent clouds. Yes: the sky is cool. Touching that piece of lunar basalt brought from a quarter-million miles away was not stranger or more marvelous to me than the touch of my sister's finger. We've all touched the moon rock. What gives us that faint interplanetary chill of awe is not the commonplace matter but the knowledge that it's come back to us from such an abyssal distance, from someplace that was torn from us long ago, a place we've always looked to with wonder and yearning, but never dreamt we would ever really go.

I'm From The Future, Asshole

1984

1995

2008

2020

Averted Vision

In 1996 I rode the Ringling Brothers circus train to Mexico City, where I lived for a month, pretending to be someone's husband. I remember my time there as we remember most of our travels—vivid and thrilling, everything new and strange. My ex-fake-wife Annie and I often reminisce nostalgically about our honeymoon there: ordering *un balde hielo* from room service to chill our Coronas every afternoon, the black velvet painting of the devil on the toilet she made me buy, our shared hilarious terror of kidnapping and murder, the giant pork rind I wrangled through customs. Which is funny, since, if I think back on it honestly, I did not actually enjoy my stay there; in fact, as *mi esposa* did not hesitate to point out at the time, I griped incessantly about the noise and stink of the city—the car horns playing shrill uptempo versions of "La Cucaracha" or the theme from *The Godfather,* the noxious mix of diesel fumes and piss. The air was so filthy we'd been there a week before I learned we had a view of the mountains.

I was similarly miserable throughout the happiest summer I ever spent in New York City. I was recovering from an affair that had ended with what are called hard feelings, and during my convalescence I was subletting a cool, airy apartment a block from Tompkins Square Park, with a kitchen window that looked out on a community garden. A theater troupe was rehearsing a production of *The Tempest* out there, and I got used to the warped rattling crash of sheet-metal thunder in the evenings. I happened to catch *The Passion of St. Joan of Arc* on cable for the first time late one night, a film I'd known nothing about—it was grotesque and beautiful, unlike anything else in cinema. (I'd had no idea there were *transcripts* of the trial of Joan of Arc.) One of the happiest memories of my life is of sitting on top of the little knoll in Tompkins Square Park with a friend, eating a sweet Hawaiian pizza and waiting to see what movie would play on the outdoor screen that was being inflated in front of us. It turned out to be *Raiders of the Lost Ark*. Even though throughout this time I was preoccupied with thoughts of the woman I'd lost and torturing myself with insane fantasies of jealousy and revenge, in retrospect it's obvious that the main thing I was doing that summer was falling in love.

I'm not sure whether it is a perversity peculiar to my own mind or just the common lot of humanity to experience happiness mostly in retrospect. I have of course considered the theory that I am an idiot who fails to appreciate anything when he actually has it and only loves what he's lost. But I think I recall that summer with such clarity and affection for much the same reason that I so pleasantly remember my month in Mexico City or even my time in Greece, where I got stabbed. Heartbreak was, in a way, like a foreign country; everything seemed fresh, brilliant, and glinting. It was as if I'd been flayed, so that even the air hurt. When you're that unhappy, any glimmer of beauty or comfort feels like running into an old friend abroad, or seeing mountaintops through smog. We mistakenly imagine we want "happiness," which we tend to picture in vague, soft-focus terms, when what we really crave is the harder-edged quality of intensity. We've all known (or been) people who returned again and again to relationships that seemed to make them miserable. Quite a few soldiers can't get used to the lowered stakes of civilian life, and reenlist. We want to be hurt, astonished, reminded we're alive. In San Francisco's Pioneer Square, Annie and I saw honeysuckle blossoms the size of lilies, their creamy fragrance filling the night air. "Are these real?" she asked.

We each have a handful of those moments, the ones we take out to treasure only rarely, like jewels, when we looked up from our lives and realized: "I'm happy." One of the last times this happened to me, inexplicably, I was driving on Maryland's unsublime Route 40 with the window down, looking at a peeling Burger King billboard while Van Halen played on the radio. But that kind of intense and present happiness is famously ephemeral; as soon as you notice it you dispel it, the way you block yourself from remembering a word by trying to retrieve it. And any attempt to contrive this feeling through some replicable method—with drinking or drugs, sexual seduction, or buying new stuff, listening to the same old songs that reliably give us shivers—never quite recaptures the spontaneous, profligate joy of the real thing. In other words, be advised that Burger King billboards and Van Halen are not a surefire combination, any more than are scotch and cigars.

About the closest approximation to happiness that we can consistently achieve by any kind of deliberate effort is the less celebrated condition of absorption. I didn't always enjoy being a cartoonist; during the twelve years of my career, if I can call it that, I bored friends and colleagues by complaining about the insulting pay, the lack of recognition, the short half-life of political cartoons as art. And yet, if I'm allowed any final accounting of my days, I may find, to my surprise, that I reckon those Fridays when I woke up without an idea in my head and only started drawing around noon, calling friends at work for emergency humor consultations, doing frantic Google image searches for *Scott McClellan* or *chacmool,* eating whatever crud was in the fridge, laughing out loud at my own inspirations, and somehow ended up getting a finished cartoon in by deadline, feeling like an evil genius and well deserving of a cold beer, to have been among my best.

If I consciously felt anything when I looked up from my work, it was mostly anxiety and guilt about having been so derelict and left everything until deadline yet again. But during the time I was actually focused on drawing—whipping out a perfect line, fluid but precise, gauging the exact cant of an eyelid to evoke an expression, or immersed in the infinitesimal universe of cross-hatching— I wasn't conscious of feeling anything at all. My senses were so integrated that, on those occasions when I had to redraw something, I often found that I would spontaneously recall the same measure of music or line of dialogue I'd been listening to when I'd drawn it the first time; the memory had become inextricably encoded in the line. It is this state that rock climbers, pinball players, and libertines are all seeking: an absorption in the immediate so intense and complete that the idiot chatter of your brain shuts up for once and you temporarily lose yourself, to your relief.

Perhaps the reason we so often experience happiness only in hindsight, and that any deliberate campaign to achieve it is so misguided, is that it isn't an obtainable goal in itself but only an aftereffect. It's the consequence of having lived in the way that we're supposed to—by which I don't mean ethically correctly but fully, consciously engaged in the business of living. In this respect it resembles averted vision, a phenomenon familiar to backyard astronomers whereby, in order to pick out a very faint star, you have to let your gaze drift casually to the space just next to it; if you look directly at it, it vanishes. And it's also true, come to think of it, that the only stars we ever see are not the real stars, those blinding cataclysms in the present, but always only the light of the untouchable past.

Notes

How They Tried to Fuck Me Over (But I Showed Them)

1. Bill Mauldin, *Up Front* (New York: Norton, 2000).

When They're Not Assholes

1. *New York Times*/CBS News Poll: "National Survey of Tea Party Supporters," April 5–12, 2010.

2. Charlie Daniels Band, "In America," *Full Moon,* 1980, Epic FE 36571.

3. John T. Jost et al., "Political Conservatism as Motivated Social Cognition: Political conservatism; psychological variables; prediction; motivated social cognition; personality; epistemic & existential needs; ideological rationalization," *Psychological Bulletin* 129:3 (2003). One of the studies cited in this survey reported that conservative women dream more frequently than liberal women about falling, being chased, and being famous, and dream less frequently about sex, a finding I'm just placing before the reader without editorial comment.

4. Ryota Kanai et al., "Political Orientations Are Correlated with Brain Structure in Young Adults," *Current Biology* 21:8 (April 2011): 677–80. Researchers cautioned that they hadn't established causality here; that is, people who are more fearful might come to have larger amygdalas rather than the other way around.

Escape from Pony Island

1. Alan Greenspan, *The Age of Turbulence: Adventures in a New World* (New York: Penguin Press, 2004), 463. "I am saddened that it is politically inconvenient to acknowledge what everyone knows: the Iraq war was largely about oil." Maybe everyone Alan Greenspan hangs out with knows this, but it would sound like the most treasonous

liberal faggotry at my local bar in rural Maryland, where freedom fries remained on the menu for a decade.

2. David Kushner, "Cormac McCarthy's Apocalypse," *Rolling Stone,* December 27, 2007.

3. Kim Stanley Robinson, *Forty Days of Rain* (New York: Bantam Books, 2004), 238.

4. Nate Hagens, "Enter the Elephant," November 15, 2009, http://campfire.theoildrum.com/node/5967.

5. Ibid.

6. Michael Anderson, director, *Logan's Run* (1976). This citation not to be construed as a recommendation.

7. Rebecca Solnit, *A Paradise Built in Hell: The Extraordinary Communities That Arise in Disaster* (New York: Viking, 2009).

8. Friedrich Nietzsche, *Human, All Too Human*, in *The Portable Nietzsche*, trans. Walter Kauffman (New York: Penguin Books, 1976), 58.

9. Joel Coen, director, *The Big Lebowski*, 1998.

10. Rebecca Solnit, 'Why Fanaticism Can Be a Good Thing,' December 1, 2009, http://www.alternet.org/story/144251/why_fanaticism_can_be_a_good_thing/.

The Referendum

1. James Salter, *Light Years* (New York: Vintage, 1995), 8.

Bad People

1. Peter A. Jay, letter to the editor, *Ægis,* August 7, 1991.

2. Ibid.

3. *Delaware State News,* August 30, 1981.

4. *Sarasota-Herald Tribune,* 26 July 1994. This story appears on the same page as an item about the attempted contract killing of a carnival performer called Lobster Boy.

Chutes and Candyland

1. James Boylan, "The Love Starter," *Remind Me to Murder You Later* (Baltimore: Johns Hopkins University Press, 1988), 84.

An Insult to the Brain

1. Friedrich Nietzsche, *Human, All Too Human,* trans. R. J. Hollingdale (Cambridge: Cambridge University Press, 1996), 238–39.

2. Cf. "Cornish Game Clams: A False Start in Five Parts," by B. Kliban, a cartoonist Mom and I both enjoyed. B. Kliban, *Two Guys Fooling Around with the Moon* (New York: Workman, 1982).

3. Lawrence Sterne, *The Life and Opinions of Tristram Shandy, Gentleman,* introduction by Christopher Morley, illustrations by T. M. Cleland (New York: Heritage Press, rept. 1935; orig pub. 1925), 102.

4. Nietzsche, *Human, All Too Human*, 239. (Nietzsche loved *Tristram Shandy.*)

5. Sterne, *Tristram Shandy*, 188.

6. Ibid., 291.

7. Ibid., 191.

8. Cf. Thomas Pynchon's syllogism: "As long as I don't sleep, he decided, I won't shave. . . . That must mean, he pursued the thought, that as soon as I fall asleep, I'll start shaving!" Thomas Pynchon, *Vineland* (Boston: Little, Brown, 1990), 160.

9. Cf. Dunbar in *Catch-22,* who tries to make every moment as boring as possible order to make his life seem to last longer. Joseph Heller, *Catch-22* (New York: Simon & Schuster Paperbacks, 1989), 9.

Sister World

1. Marilynne Robinson, *Gilead* (New York: Picador, 2004), 136.

Acknowledgments

The way that you write a book is to cultivate friendships with people who are smarter, funnier, saner, and wiser than you, and then steal everything they say. Both this book and I are better than they would have been without the benefit of my conversations and correspondence with Chris Beck, Jim and Jenny Boylan, Claire, Emma, and Susan Connolly, David Dudley, Jim Fisher, Michelle Gienow, Sarah Glidden, Myla Goldberg, Nell Greenfieldboyce, Lisa Gwilliam, Lisa Hanawalt, Tom Hart, Dave Israel, Megan Kelso, Libby Kessman, Mildred Kreider, Steve McLoughlin, John Patton, Matt Taibbi, Bart Taylor, Ellen Twaddell, the evil Ben Walker, and Boyd White. Thanks in particular to Myla, Megan, Ellen, and Boyd for serving as my readers. I also owe thanks to Hope Lassen for her research and to Ray Villard of the Hubble Space Telescope Institute for his consultation.

It is also helpful to have a team of professionals whose job is to ensure that your book does not suck. I was fortunate to have two astute editors, Alessandra Bastagli and Amber Qureshi, to whom I am deeply indebted. Thanks also to Sydney Tanigawa for her advice. Peter Catapano of the *New York Times* gave me a forum and unerring editorial guidance for the earliest of these essays. I would never have undertaken to draw the cartoon essay "The Stabbing Story" had David Dudley not commissioned it. And inexpressible thanks are due to my agent, Meg Thompson, without whom I might still be a cartoonist.

My Dirty Little Secrets

I ACTUALLY DO KIND OF LIKE SOME CHILDREN.

I AM NOW AND THEN STRICKEN BY A POIGNANT AND MOURNFUL FONDNESS FOR MY FELLOW MAN.

I'M A LITTLE BUNNY RABBIT.

SOMETIMES I THINK MAYBE EVERYTHING'S GOING TO BE FINE.

About the Author

Tim Kreider was born and educated in Baltimore. His cartoon *The Pain—When Will It End?* ran in the Baltimore *City Paper* for twelve years, and has been collected in three books published by Fantagraphics. His writing has appeared in the *New York Times, Film Quarterly,* the *Comics Journal*, and on nerve.com. He divides his time between New York City and the Chesapeake Bay.